Michael Grose is one of Australia's leading parenting and educational writers and speakers. He is the author of nine books for
parents, including *Why First Borns Rule the World* and *Thriving!*
Currently he supports over 1500 schools in Australia and
internationally to build strong partnerships with their parent
communities.

Michael was recently elevated to the PSA Speaker Hall of Fame
when he won the Educator Award for Excellence. He was the
first person to conduct a parenting seminar for a nation's leaders,
when he ventured into Parliament House, Canberra, in 2004 and
addressed politicians on both sides of the political fence about
how to behave so your children will too!

For more information and practical ideas on parenting visit his
website: www.parentingideas.com.au.

SPOONFED GENERATION

How to raise independent children

MICHAEL GROSE

BANTAM

SYDNEY AUCKLAND TORONTO NEW YORK LONDON

A Bantam book
Published by Penguin Random House Australia Pty Ltd
Level 3, 100 Pacific Highway, North Sydney NSW 2060
www.penguin.com.au

Penguin
Random House
Australia

First published by Bantam in 2017

Addresses for the Penguin Random House group of companies can be found at
global.penguinrandomhouse.com/offices.

National Library of Australia
Cataloguing-in-Publication entry

Grose, Michael, 1955– author
Spoonfed generation/Michael Grose

ISBN 978 0 14378 104 2 (paperback)

Parent and child
Parenting
Child rearing
Discipline of children
Self-confidence in children

Cover illustration by Westend61, courtesy of Getty Images
Cover design by Josh Durham
Internal design by Midland Typesetters, Australia
Typeset in 12/16.5 pt Berkeley LT by Midland Typesetters, Australia
Printed in Australia by Griffin Press, an accredited ISO AS/NZS 14001:2004
Environmental Management System printer

Penguin Random House Australia uses papers that are natural, renewable
and recyclable products and made from wood grown in sustainable forests.
The logging and manufacturing processes are expected to conform to the
environmental regulations of the country of origin.

For Sam, Emma and Sarah.
Love watching you parent now.

Contents

Prologue

Currently we do too much for our kids. We give them too much, expect too little, and are raising a generation of nervous children who fall apart when a skerrick of pressure is applied to them.

Should we be worried? Yes, we should!

One in three girls and one in five boys in Australia now live with an anxiety disorder. That's unprecedented. It shouldn't be happening in a prosperous country like ours, yet the statistics are there for all to see.

What has given rise to this epidemic of anxiety that's gripping our kids, making them fearful to navigate their neighbourhoods as their parents once did, leading them to avoid learning opportunities at school and restrict the possibilities open to them? The world certainly feels like a more dangerous place – with the twenty-four-hour news cycle that graphically brings atrocities from around the world into our living rooms and heightens feelings of fear and helplessness. This fear is impacting our kids and the way we raise them, making them more dependent on their parents than was the case with previous generations.

Why are kids so fearful?

Our spoonfeeding ways mean we are raising a generation of risk-averse kids who are incapable of making decisions without deferring to a parent, sibling or peer lest they make a mistake; who can't make their lunch or cook a meal; who need a parent to defend them when a teacher speaks to them tersely; and who remain reliant financially and emotionally on their parents well into their twenties. Never before has a generation been so dependent on their parents; now it's time to remove the spoon and put it back in the drawer.

Independence-building has always been the cornerstone of effective parenting, but over the past few decades we've lost our way. While parents mean well by protecting their kids it's better in the long term to teach them to solve their problems rather than resolve all their difficulties for them.

The story behind this story

'You want to go where? You want to go for how long?'

My eldest daughter, at the age of fifteen, announced that she wanted to go to Denmark on a six-month student-exchange program. I wasn't prepared for such a request, but clearly she was. Her announcement took me by surprise because Emma was just halfway through her secondary schooling. She was doing well academically, however I was aware that she was having some friendship problems. But what teenage girl wasn't, I thought to myself. Situation normal.

My daughter's Denmark Proclamation shook me out of my lethargy. Was she ready for such a trip? How would she cope being away from her family for such a long period? Didn't she know that she wouldn't get any visitors from home when she was on the other side of the world? Did she know what she was doing?

After the initial shock, my wife Sue and I decided to support her trip with one proviso – she had to drive the whole project herself. Not only was this a test of her resolve, but it was also proof that she would be able to function without her parents. Her ability to organise all facets of the trip, from sourcing a suitable program to getting a visa and taking care of every other detail, was going to stand her in good stead while she was away. As it proved, she passed this test with flying colours and some months later with moist eyes, heavy hearts and much parental pride my wife Sue and I waved our daughter, then sixteen, off on her six-month sojourn more than 10,000 kilometres away in another hemisphere. I couldn't believe she was so capable. But I wasn't ready for her to go. I couldn't believe she didn't need me any more. I felt, well, not quite discarded, but . . . redundant. For the next six months she wouldn't rely on her family to provide her everyday needs; to be daily emotional supports; to coach and coax her when she had social difficulties; to chauffeur her to sports and leisure activities, friends' homes and parties. At fifteen, like most of her contemporaries, she was some way off adulthood but she was making giant leaps in that direction and possessed many of the tools as well as the motivation needed to make the transition from adolescence to adulthood. As parents I figured we must have done something right.

Failure to launch

In contrast, many young adults currently face enormous difficulty when transitioning into the next phase of development – a stage that involves greater independence and responsibility. Dubbed the 'failure to launch syndrome' after the 2006 Matthew McConaughey film of the same name, it refers to the increasing number of young people who may have left school but haven't transitioned to the next stage of development – adulthood. They are stuck in a netherworld between adulthood and adolescence – not quite adults and no longer teenagers, these failure-to-launch kids depend on their parents for emotional and social support, well into their twenties, and in some cases beyond.

This failure to launch can be attributed to a multitude of reasons, including lack of rites of passage that act as natural signals for both parents and young people that they are moving away from the family nest and into another life phase. Many experts attribute this failure to launch to the current educational climate where students are spoonfed, or at least given every possible assistance to get them over the educational line. Once they leave school many find that there is a significant mismatch between the real world of work and their experience of school. In short, their schools may have prepared them very successfully to pass examinations but failed woefully to prepare them for anything beyond the examination room. Add to this an overprotective style of parenting where parents step in to rescue their children from a failing grade, an unfinished paper, or a disciplinary consequence, and it's little wonder that young people remain heavily dependent on their families for longer than occurred in previous generations.

Out they go!

I read with amusement the headline of a recent article published in a major Australian newspaper: 'Why parents should kick their adult children out of home' (Gab Doquile, brisbanetimes.com.au, 9 April 2016). The writer lamented the fact that many of her contemporaries were currently doting on young adults who were living at home rent- and responsibility-free while studying or working compared to her own experience of leaving home at seventeen. A parent of two sons who at the time of writing were in Years 9 and 11, she was determined to show them the front door once they left secondary school. While she is a parent after my own heart I couldn't help thinking that young people don't magically develop these coping skills and resilience simply because they leave home or reach a certain age. In fact, the readiness to transition from adolescence to adulthood and away from dependence on parents begins in early childhood. This is the stage immediately following infancy when kids are almost totally dependent on their parents and carers to meet most of their physical needs. During early childhood (around fifteen to eighteen months) kids are on the move and suddenly want to do everything for themselves. The wish for independence is paramount, and it's during this stage that parents can begin to lay the foundations for real independence, which comes some years later.

Ready for launch

So, at fifteen was Emma ready to launch into the world of adulthood? Not entirely; she was moving from the cocoon of her family of origin and its comfortable familiarity to the safety net of another family, albeit in another hemisphere. Apart from the clues picked up from a sketchy bio and some family happy snaps, her new family was largely an unknown quantity. However, the fact that she was willing to go was an indication of her readiness. Her ability to drive the project and overcome the organisational hurdles along the way offered a small measure of proof also that she was ready and able to go. But her preparedness to leave was no accident. A combination of factors meant that she was well placed to not just survive but to thrive in an unfamiliar environment away from her family and friends for such a significant time.

Her gender helped. Being a girl meant she had a natural head start in organisational ability and social maturity over many boys of the same age. I dare say, many of the boys in her social group at the same age would have had difficulty finding the airport let alone negotiating the details of the trip. Her personality type also offered two distinct advantages. She had an easy-going, flexible temperament that enabled her to go with the flow and feel at ease with uncertainty. She was also a gregarious, outgoing girl who easily initiated social contact and knew how to make and, importantly, keep friends. We thought that all things being equal she should have little trouble forming new family ties and making new friendships abroad.

Her birth order position was also in her favour. As the middle of three children she had the advantage of the outward orientation that comes from being squeezed between two children. She didn't have the perks and privileges that come from being the eldest, nor did she get the easy life afforded the youngest. Not only did she have to fend for herself more than the others, but like many middle children she looked outside her family to gain a sense of belonging and acceptance. As I wrote in *Why First Borns Rule the World and Last Borns Want to Change It*, middle-born children, or those with a middle-born orientation, are almost always the first to flee the family nest. Emma was a case in point, though she left a great deal earlier than we expected.

Her upbringing had also prepared her well for her trip. She was purposefully raised with independence and resilience in mind. She was brought up by parents who lived the notion of *Never regularly do anything for a child that they can do for themselves.* That type of mantra runs off the lips easily but takes some effort and determination to carry out. It means you have to stand back and allow children and young people the time and opportunity to develop a range of self-help skills, from tying shoelaces, to making school lunches and organising transport to after-school activities. It means you've got to resist the very real temptation to rescue them when they continually forget things such as school lunches. It means also that you have to be strong and resist their inclination to transfer their problems such as being late to school over to you. The many facets of independence are crucial in preparing kids for negotiating situations away from the family home.

Helping our daughter and her siblings cope with life's curve balls was central to our parenting, playing no small part in Emma's readiness to manage the loneliness, homesickness and the unknown elements of the environment in which she was entering. Resilience refers to the twofold notion of helping kids cope when life becomes difficult and the longer-term view of developing strengths and capacities to manage future hardships, and it is best promoted when it becomes the prime mindset of parents, carers and teachers. Emma's educational experiences had prepared her well for significant time away from home. In particular, a very tough ten-day Outward Bound camp the previous year had taught her some fabulous skills and mindsets such as *Just get through the day when things get tough*, which she drew on when she was away.

As it turned out, the style of parenting that Emma and her siblings received, more by accident than good design, prepared her for this earlier than expected launch. Much of our parenting was aimed at removing ourselves in a management and emotional sense so that our children learned to stand on their own two feet at the earliest possible age. This focus on self-reliance gave her the confidence she needed to leave home.

So, what is this book about?

This book is a how-to guide for parents to raise confident, resilient, independent kids who are ready to launch; not necessarily at fifteen, though that's a possibility. I will show you how you can raise your kids so they are ready to negotiate life outside school, including relationships, and to pursue their vocation with a purpose and motivation. It's a guide to removing the fear from kids' lives so that they can make the most of the chances that come their way rather than shrink or withdraw when life places expectations on them. The premise of this book is that children have a natural inclination to launch – some take longer than others and, if I keep the analogy going, some will crash land along the way. But it's in the landing that many lessons are learned. In effect, childhood and adolescence is a series of take-offs and crash landings that prepare kids for life outside the family nest.

This is a book about you!

Equipping kids with the skills and knowledge they need to leave home has ramifications for parents too. The flip side of independence-building is that parents invariably make themselves redundant in a managerial sense. Many parents I meet feel quite uncomfortable with this idea. It's certainly not something any parent thinks about when they hold a baby in their arms. The urge to love and be loved is overwhelming with children in infancy. However, as infancy gives way to early childhood, then childhood (latency) and eventually adolescence, parents need to embrace the idea that their children become less reliant on them. At some stage every parent becomes redundant, at least in a managerial and emotional sense, as their children become increasingly self-sufficient. This is a book about parenting redundancy as much as it's a book about raising kids with the skills, tools and mindsets that will help them become self-sufficient when they leave school (rather than sometime around their late twenties, which seems to be the new norm).

Let's read more.

Introduction:
What keeps kids so
dependent?

Let's start with the big question: What age would you like your child to be able to leave home?

This is a challenging question for many parents. It's an easy one for me to ask because my adult children have all successfully flown the family nest, established their own families and forged their own lives independent of me. I suspect if that question had been posed when my eldest was three years old I would have said, 'When they're twenty-one,' which two decades ago was still a recognised marker of adulthood. I may have even used education or employment as a marker, saying something like, 'When they've finished school or tertiary studies they'll finally be out of my hair.' But in truth I don't think that was a question I ever really spent much time thinking about. Like most parents of young children my wife Sue and I were just trying to get

1

through each day; we didn't spend much time looking at the bigger picture.

In hindsight I probably underestimated my children's capabilities. If asked this question now I would confidently give a more definite answer: 'I'd like my kids to be able to leave home at fifteen.' I suspect most parents reading this would throw their hands up in protest. They'd look around at the teenagers in their lives, many of whom are either dissenters or just plain difficult to raise, and would come to only one conclusion – 'They're not ready! They won't be ready to leave home for a long time!' And they may be right. Adolescence is a turbulent time with many young people fighting their own physiology, but that doesn't mean that they couldn't manage and organise their own lives if they had to.

Developmentally, fifteen- and sixteen-year-olds are getting ready to fly the parenting nest. Boys are programmed to fight with their fathers at this age, and many dads I know if they gave way to their emotions would gladly oblige and tip them out. Girls also are programmed for dissent, often pushing their parents away in a quest for greater autonomy and freedom. But our current community is not programmed for such early departures. And in past millennia that is exactly what fathers did, with boys generally starting work, taking up apprenticeships or even leaving home in their mid teen years. Girls, on the other hand, tended to stay home a little longer because they didn't reach puberty until sixteen or seventeen; they were, however, capable enough in practical terms to look after themselves away from the family nest.

Today's kids stay home longer

It's well established that young people in Western countries such as Australia, many parts of Europe, and the United States, as well as Asian counterparts including Japan, are still at home well into their twenties and, in some cases, beyond their twenties. The reasons are many and varied, including: lack of employment opportunities, longer time spent in education, high rents and lack of housing affordability. Certainly young people are currently financially dependent on their parents for longer than in previous generations; and it would be safe to say that the situation won't change much in the coming decades, with current economic indicators suggesting that life for young people may not be as economically rosy as it was for Baby Boomers – but that doesn't mean that young people should be tied to their parents' apron strings into their twenties and beyond. This extended dependence means that parents delay their retirements as funds that previous generations would have put aside for their retirements are diverted to support their adult children.

Letting go of ties that bind

The challenge for parents is to raise their kids so they are capable of looking after themselves at the age of fifteen. If you have a boy, this may take longer because gender plays a part in the maturation process. In my book XYZ I wrote about the advent of adultescence, the new breed of twentysomething stuck in a netherworld between adolescence and adulthood still heavily reliant on their parents and other adults. Anecdotally, it seems many young men choose to avoid donning the badge of adulthood until their mid to late twenties. The early twenties is, it seems for many young men, a time of experimentation where they move from course to course, or from job to job, after taking a gap year or three. All this while they have the safe haven of their original family to return to if life were to go awry.

Dependency relationships are unhealthy

There are two types of relationships – those that encourage dependency and those that seek redundancy by ensuring that neither person is dependent on the other. While it can be argued that there are times when a dependency relationship is permissible, such as when a child is enduring a long illness, I'm not sure that dependency relationships between adults and children are healthy in the long term. Parents, teachers and carers should always do as much as possible to get out of the way and allow children to develop the competencies and confidence to become independent. This requires adults to revert to their primary role as teacher, which takes skill, effort and time to achieve. Adults encourage dependency by rescuing children from most of their problems; by doing too much for them; by making decisions for them; and by neglecting to develop the very skills and competencies that will enable them to reach real independence. The current propensity to micro-manage doesn't serve children or young people well; it only keeps them dependent on adults for longer.

Making independence happen

Maurice Balson, the Australian parenting pioneer and author of *Becoming Better Parents*, was fond of telling aspiring teachers and parent educators, 'Never regularly do for a child the things a child can do for himself.' This simple sentence takes some unpicking. It's probably the original parenting-for-independence manifesto, and it's a philosophy that guided me when raising my three children. In effect, for me, this sentence meant that wherever possible I gave my children the skills and competencies to look after themselves physically and emotionally. It required a great deal of patience, time and courage. It also required me to be aware of the parenting requirements of the different developmental stages, all of which I will discuss in this book.

Parenting for independence takes patience

Getting kids ready for launch takes patience, because independence-building is a significant educative process. And developing new skills and abilities, whether learning how to prepare a snack or setting an alarm to get up each morning, means that kids will make lots of mistakes. Errors are part and parcel of any education process. After preparing their snack they'll leave a mess in the kitchen. Inevitably, they'll sleep in at times because they forgot to set the alarm. These mistakes don't mean that we discontinue our independence-building drive. However, it's these types of mistakes that prevent many parents from delegating tasks to their kids. Instead parents need to be patient and give kids time to master their newly developing skills.

Parenting for independence is time-consuming

Parenting for self-reliance and independence takes time. Any parent who has taught a preschooler to tie their shoelaces will know the frustration of racing out the door in the morning only to be held up by a child determined to tie their own laces. A thirty-second job for a parent can take a young child five minutes or more. Time is a commodity that most parents lack, so invariably they will tie their child's shoelaces, or alternatively, buy them Velcro shoes. It takes time to teach kids new skills and support their learning. It also takes time to encourage children to develop new skills. But by not taking the time to develop independence we discourage children from becoming independent.

Redundancy parenting sends a message to kids: *I know you are capable, so I'm going to give you the time you need to develop new competencies.* Dependency parenting, on the other hand, sends the message to kids: *I don't think you can do this so I'll do it myself.* Of course, the message of inadequacy that dependency parenting sends has a habit of sticking, which may account for the astonishingly high number of smart but low-risk-taking kids we now see in our school systems.

Parenting for independence takes courage

Above all, parenting for self-reliance takes a great deal of courage. It's relatively easy to develop independence in kids when they are in the safe confines of home.

- Prepare your own breakfast, Mr 4 Year Old. What's the worst that can happen? A broken plate or spilled milk.
- Get yourself ready for school, Miss 9 Year Old. What's the worst that can happen? Late for school and risk the teacher's displeasure.
- Organise your own homework routine, Mr 14 Year Old. What's the worst that can happen? Get homework in late or not at all.

In each example parents need courage, because no one wants to see their child fail. Not to mention that children's failures and poor choices can reflect upon them as parents. Parenting for independence requires you to separate yourself from your child. But these risks are minor compared to the risks that come with granting independence outside the home as there are many variables which parents can't control. It takes courage to allow primary-school children to walk or ride home from school even though you have vetted the journey for any obvious dangers and gone over the route with them. It takes courage to allow an early teen to take public transport to go to the cinema or into the city with friends even though they've travelled that route many times with you. It takes courage to allow a mid teen to go to a party with young people his own age, even though you know that there will be adult supervision. These risks always seem heightened when it involves our first child because we tend to be in new ground, and are always uncertain of their readiness. Parents often underestimate their children's capabilities, while children often overestimate them. It's tricky finding middle ground.

Parenting for independence is important

Why is independence so important for kids? There are many ways to approach this question, but I'd prefer to take a developmental perspective. It has always been a biological imperative to raise children to become independent of their parents, but over time there have been many different layers added to child-rearing, which have pushed us toward a style of parenting that encourages dependence on parents rather than independence. The move to smaller families is a significant factor. In small families parents are better positioned to do everything for kids, whereas in larger families (families of four or more children) parents delegate more. When time is in short supply, there is a natural tendency to do things for kids instead of allowing them to do for themselves – we just want life to be smooth sailing, so it's easier to do rather than delegate and take the risk of having an argument, managing a tantrum or fixing a child's mistakes if they muck up.

The high level of anxiety surrounding child-rearing at present is absolutely stifling and unwarranted, and inhibits parents' ability to develop independence in children. Most parents I encounter admit that their children don't enjoy the same freedom to move around their neighbourhood as they had as children. Even though they recognise that freedom was a positive for them, most cite fear as the factor that prevents them granting their children the same freedom and hence more independence.

Finally, over the past two decades society has lifted the status of parenting to the top of the pedestal of power and influence on a child, and this is a massive factor behind the shift toward dependency. While it may be ironic for a parenting author to state that parenting is over-rated, I believe that by seeing parenting as the primary influencer for children we devalue the influence of peers, broader family, teachers and other adults on children's lives. Jeffrey Kluger, author of *The Sibling Effect*, reminds us that the sibling relationship in many instances is more influential than the parent–child relationship. His wonderful book highlights the lasting impact that siblings can have on each other. I don't wish to discount a parent's influence on children – it is immense – but it is not the only factor in determining a child's outcomes.

I'm not proposing we practise benign neglect, whereby we pay less attention to children and give them space, thus providing opportunities to develop the skills and wherewithal to stand on their own two feet from the youngest possible age. Parents should be more strategic than that. I'm not suggesting that we ignore children or leave them to their own devices when the family is a small one. This smacks of under-parenting, which causes many problems for kids. Nor am I suggesting over-parenting, where we become too involved by overseeing the minutiae of children's lives. Rather we need to seek a middle ground where parents are mindful of the need to grant children space and opportunity to develop a range of skills needed for independent living, but within the modern context of families generally having two or fewer children and time being at a premium, as well as one, not always two, parents doing the child-rearing.

So, let's keep moving.

part one

Independence

'Mum, you forgot to pack my lunch this morning.' What's wrong with this statement?

It's a dependency statement. This child has given responsibility to his mother for packing his lunch. This may be suitable in some circumstances, such as if a child has additional needs, or if a child is feeling under stress because they are doing exams or they're being bullied. In those circumstances parents should ease the load for kids by taking some of their responsibilities away. But in normal circumstances most children of school age are quite capable of packing their own school lunches. We parents so often take on the responsibility for children's problems, which increases kids' dependence on us.

As I stated at the start of this book, independence needs to be our goal for our children. I stress that this is *our* goal for children, because they won't necessarily buy in to the independence dream just because you want them to. You'll need to work hard and be determined if you're going to develop independence in each of your children.

Most parents I speak with want their children to become independent. It's a no-brainer really. They want their children to be able to make their own choices, to think for themselves and to embrace responsibility. Yet our current parenting style is depriving children of independence rather than promoting it.

chapter one

The importance of independence

What's holding us back?

As revealed recently on the excellent ABC television program *Life at 9* (which has followed the development of a group of Australian children over two-year periods since they were one), most nine-year-olds don't feel ready to embrace independence.

Paradoxically, one of the main reasons for this is that parents often limit the development of their children's independence. For instance, in one experiment children and their mothers built something together: in every mother–child pairing it was the parent who took the lead and made the decisions about what they should build. Later, when children were given the chance to build alone, they universally preferred their own construction over the one they co-created with their mother. Self-esteem is built when children do things on their own, not when things are done for them.

On the responsibility front, less than 50 per cent of the nine-year-olds in the series do regular chores. However, 90 per cent of children who grow up in large families do things such as get themselves ready for school and help around the house. Disturbingly, most of the nine-year-olds in the study thought the world was a dangerous place. Fear of strangers, increased traffic and the sheer size of suburban neighbourhoods mean today's nine-year-olds spend more time in the car than walking around their local area. Three in four children are driven to school, whereas just a generation ago that number was more like one in three.

Keeping kids safe from harm and free from responsibility can prevent them from learning, and stop them from thinking for themselves. The more children move away from parent protection the more they move toward dealing with adversity and, importantly, autonomy.

Developmentally, nine is the age when children should be getting out of their comfort zone. It's an age when kids need the freedom to flourish, within the context of parental nurturing and monitoring to provide the safety necessary for healthy autonomy. Generally the nurturing and monitoring is already in place; what is needed is an increase in what kids are expected to do for themselves. After all, life will eventually place these expectations on them, so they need to practise self-reliance in the safe confines of childhood.

Size and time matter too

In large families independence happens naturally. If you were born into a large brood you more than likely didn't have a parent on hand all the time to help you with the day-to-day activities of living. It was more likely that you relied on the help of a sibling, whether it was to get you out of bed each morning, remind you to pack a bag, help look for those lost socks, or just hurry you along to school. Otherwise, you were probably left to your own devices where you learned to fend for yourself. Experience, both bitter and sweet, became one of your main teachers. But large families today are rare. With families of two children being the most common, the development of independence in kids can be harder to achieve.

Lack of time means that we often don't afford children the learning opportunities they need. Children and young people will invariably make mistakes, be forgetful and do things poorly, but this doesn't mean that parents shouldn't grant these opportunities. It does mean that we need to be patient and allow them the time to gain mastery over their own lives. It also means that we need to be prepared for children to operate at their own level for a time rather than quickly reach lofty heights of adult expectations.

The many faces of independence

'I can do it!'

At the time of writing, this is one of the favourite phrases of my four-year-old granddaughter. Efforts to get her out of her car seat; to put her in the bath; endeavour to get her dressed in the morning and a myriad of other activities are all met with those four words. They are accompanied by a steely determination to go it alone that if stymied can result in her letting you know in no uncertain terms that 'I can do it MYSELF!' This type of scenario, well known to most parents, is indicative of many children of this age. Independence is the default mechanism as physically they become increasingly able to gain mastery over their world. Whereas in infancy they were completely dependent on their parents to take care of most of their physical needs, they reach a stage where *I can do it!* becomes an enticing possibility. It is so important as a parent to channel, even encourage, a child's attempts to become independent at this stage, because this is the age when the road to independence can be either opened up for kids or closed down by the roadblocks of impatience, overindulgence, fear and lack of time.

Let's look at what independence looks like and how we can create opportunities for kids to become independent.

Look after yourself (becoming capable)

Independence takes many forms but perhaps the most common is the development of self-help skills. For very young children self-help means feeding themselves, dressing and undressing, washing their hands, cleaning their teeth and the like. The simplest way to understand the extent of self-help skills is to start from a child's body and work outwards from there. As children grow more toward school age and beyond, their world expands and so too does their range of self-help skills. So, feeding yourself as a toddler extends to preparing your own breakfast, making simple snacks and eventually to cooking your own meals in late primary school. The confidence, pride and, for most, sheer pleasure that kids get from this type of self-mastery is immeasurable. Yet it is so easily denied by well-meaning parents and adults who see it as their job to do everything for children. Independence begins at home with the development of self-help skills.

The *Never regularly do for a child the things a child can do for themselves* mantra has many variations but they all come to the same conclusion – when a child can do something, let them do

16

it! That's okay in theory, but of course the busy lifestyles that most parents live today mean that compromises must be made. There are times when you need to dress your child quickly rather than wait while they fumble their way into their clothes, particularly when work, childcare and school deadlines must be met. However, if you are always dressing your child rather than this being the exception, it is safe to say you are thwarting a child's efforts to become independent.

Unconditional acceptance

Here's a dilemma. One day after school you ask your six-year-old to tidy up his bedroom. (You have the reasonable belief that it's his room, so he should keep it tidy.) He tries his best to clean it but you look around and you see that his standards of tidiness differ from yours. There are toys sticking out from under his bed, he has parked half a dozen toy cars on his desk and has placed his folded pyjamas on top of his pillow instead of under it. This isn't what you had in mind, but your son is happy with his room and you know he has done his best. He's not pulling the proverbial wool over your eyes. What to do? Should you go in and tidy the room to your liking? Should you ask your son to have another go because it's not good enough? Should you congratulate him for keeping his room neat and tidy? How should you respond?

Interesting question. It helps to understand a powerful concept first before answering. That is, if you are going to develop self-help skills in children, it is important to practise a simple concept called unconditional acceptance. You need to accept your child's best efforts at bed-making, bedroom tidiness, preparing a meal or whatever task you've given them according to their age and stage of development. In this example, the creative room tidy of

Mr 6 may be the very best he can do. However, the same child at ten may need to lift his game a little. If your child's independence is your goal, don't go into their room and redo it to your lofty standards – even though it may make you feel better seeing an organised bedroom. Do this and a child will think, *Why bother? Do it yourself next time.* Far better and smarter to accept this effort unconditionally and perhaps compromise by tidying the room yourself once a week or joining your child in some of his tidy sessions so you can help him learn some of the tricks of the tidiness game.

Birth order counts

Eldest children usually have a head start in the self-help stakes. The expectation for them to fend for themselves is generally higher than for other birth-order positions. When coupled with the likelihood that they often help, and at times teach, a younger sibling to take care of themselves, it is little wonder that many eldest children are extremely self-sufficient. Youngest children, on the other hand, have a knack of putting other people in their service. They tend to outsource their self-help skills to anyone who is willing to help, often an eldest born, so the so-called baby of the family – who can also be a second-born – frequently lags behind in the self-sufficiency stakes. It can be argued, though, that what they lack in self-sufficiency skills they more than make up for in charm, and persuasion skills, so this group never lacks for much.

Gender matters

Gender shouldn't matter when it comes to development of self-help skills, but it does, particularly within certain cultures. For instance, after spending four months in Italy recently this writer noticed that girls were far more skilled at looking after themselves than were boys in the same family. This mismatch can be put down to one factor – boys were not expected to help out around the home, nor to do a great deal to look after themselves. The mothers generally look after their sons so well that most Italian men are still in the family home in their mid to late twenties; and they won't leave until they find a partner (and mother replacement) and form their own family. Girls, on the other hand, are expected to help with general household duties as well as keep their bedrooms clean, prepare their own school meals and place their own clothes in the washing basket. All good training for becoming mother replacements and looking after the men in their lives later on.

Cultural and societal norms play a huge part in child-rearing. Perhaps nowhere is it as tangible and significant than the matter of developing the skills of self-sufficiency. This begs the question: does self-sufficiency matter? It *does* matter, because relationships become tedious when one person is dependent on the other to meet their daily needs. In modern Western cultures where often both parents in a two-parent family work, this means the load is not always shared equally. One parent invariably does a double-shift, which becomes a family norm that is repeated down the line. Also, anecdotal evidence suggests that one person holds an unhealthy level of power over the other in a dependency relationship. The power built on dominance or around guilt ensures that the status quo – a dependency relationship – will continue unabated. As my granddaughter of the *I'll do it myself* variety reminds me, self-sufficiency is a very liberating thing, particularly when you are a child. Finally, you get to experience the exhilaration that comes from mastery over some of the basic functions that make up daily life. But it is also liberating from a relationship point of view because it allows people to co-exist independently without the baggage that comes with one person being reliant on the other.

Take responsibility

Many years ago I took Sarah, my youngest daughter, to preschool, where I received a first-class lesson in developing children's responsibility. The preschool teacher met us in the foyer and asked Sarah to put her book in the library bag. As quick as a flash Sarah said, 'Daddy forgot to pack it!'

The preschool teacher promptly replied, 'Sarah, I didn't ask your dad. I asked *you*!' The big lesson staring me in the face was that to develop responsibility in children, first you had to give them responsibility. And that's exactly what the teacher had done.

The teacher gave me some advice to steer me from my spoon-feeding ways. 'Your job is to make it easy for her to remember, but not to take the responsibility away.' So, in practical terms I reminded Sarah after reading her book to place it by the front door so she would remember it on the way out – but it was up to Sarah to put it in her bag on the way out. Fortunately, when she forgot, her teacher showed her displeasure to Sarah rather than blame me for being a poor parent. Often we step in as parents and take responsibility for many issues and problems that belong to children because we don't want to be considered bad parents by others.

Allow kids to own their problems

Recently, a father confessed that he struggled to get his fourteen-year-old son out of bed each morning. It took him at least three reminders before he finally drew back the sheets and demanded his son get out of bed. My advice was straightforward: don't wake him; let him get himself out of bed. Mr 14 was never going to worry about getting up while his dad did all the fretting. The dad, rather than the son, was responsible for him getting up. Instead, the father needed to give the problem over to the person who should own it – the fourteen-year-old – and stand back and allow him to accept responsibility for his actions.

Giving responsibility can mean managing mess-ups

The trouble with delegating responsibility to kids is that inevitably many children and young people will make mistakes. They'll leave school lunches at home, which may mean people cast aspersions on your ability to care for your child. They'll forget to put the rubbish bins out on garbage night, meaning your bin will be overflowing for the next week. They'll make poor choices when they use their pocket money, spending it all on the first day leaving them with nothing for the rest of the week. Accepting responsibility is a learning curve. Kids inevitably won't get things right the first time, but that doesn't mean we should stop giving them responsibilities as well as problems to solve.

Experience is a fabulous teacher. For some children, and almost all teenage boys, experience is their best teacher. These experiential learners often learn the hard way. Sometimes it takes many lessons until the learning takes hold, which can be difficult for parents who with the benefit of experience can easily foresee difficulties ahead. So, it takes a brave parent to give responsibility to a child or young person, knowing that they may struggle for a time. The other side of the coin is to give kids some responsibility – say, for getting up in the morning

21

and getting to school on time – only to rescue them – by driving them to school if they're late – or worse, make excuses for them or blame yourself. This only makes you – rather than your child – responsible for their behaviour. Developing responsibility in kids is a two-fold process – giving them some real jobs, real tasks and real problems to solve and then allowing them to experience the consequences of either decision-making, forgetfulness or lacklustre performance. The lessons are usually found in the mistakes and mess-ups. The real learning occurs in the recovery or fine-tuning that follows to minimise mistakes next time.

Expand your horizons

Independence is built when children spend time in unpredictable circumstances and environments, such as in the bush or through navigating their neighbourhoods on their own. In 2009 Lenore Skenazy, a New York journalist, wrote a book called *Free-Range Kids*, which encouraged American parents to throw open their front doors and get their kids outside playing and moving around their neighbourhoods. She was highly criticised at the time for allowing her nine-year-old son to catch the New York subway on his own. It was ironic that Skenazy was criticised for encouraging parents to give their children the same freedom that they more than likely enjoyed as children. She now has a healthy following as more parents rightfully embrace her mantra of allowing kids greater freedom to move around their neighbourhoods without adult accompaniment.

Most parents of my generation and the generation that followed enjoyed carefree childhoods where they could travel around their towns and suburbs with ease. They generally speak fondly of experiences such as walking or riding bikes to visit friends, spending time in streets and parks with a mate or catching public transport to a nearby town to take in a movie or just hang around with friends. Yet most parents won't afford their children the same freedoms, despite the fact they recognise that these were important childhood experiences. There is a tremendous desire today for parents to keep their children safe, but in doing so this robs them of many great learning experiences.

With freedom comes unpredictability

It's easy to be nostalgic about the past. The good times tend to be magnified and the bad times forgotten. When adults look back wistfully at their childhood freedoms it's the fun times they remember not the close shaves or the brushes with danger they may have experienced. I know that when I really examine my childhood – and I enjoyed a great deal of freedom – there are some memories that make me shudder. Diving off the ten-metre tower at the local swimming pool well before I was ready. Playing football alongside a four-lane highway. Riding my bike without lights through busy streets at night. These are just the tamer stories I'm prepared to put into print. Many people, I suspect, would have a similar bag of memories too. Here's the point: it was the edgier escapades rather than the safe experiences that shaped me, and made me less fearful as a child. It was the time spent climbing walls, scampering across drains, exploring abandoned warehouses, racing billy carts that I'd built myself down a hill, and building cubbies out of scraps that I'd scrounged from a nearby wood yard that stick out in my memory. It was these adventures away from adult supervision that taught me so much about being resourceful, about accessing risk and also about confronting my fears. These experiences, which can be filed under Mucking Around, were great for building confidence and curiosity in a young boy. Unfortunately, these are not the type of experiences that many of today's children enjoy.

The great outdoors is great for kids' confidence levels

Getting kids outside is perhaps one of the biggest challenges for modern parents, particularly in urban settings. Yet the outdoors is where adventure and unpredictability can be found.

It seems that girls benefit enormously in terms of self-esteem and self-confidence when they spend time in activities, including sports, outdoor play and camping. Author Gisela Preuschoff, in her book *Raising Girls*, describes a longitudinal study that showed how girls are generally more fearful than boys. The physical signs of fear, including increased heart rate and enlarged pupils, are more prevalent in girls than in boys.

There is probably some physiological reason for this, as androgens (male hormones) have a calming effect, which causes boys to feel less fear. However, Jerome Kagan, Professor of Psychology at Harvard University, believes that excessive fear in girls is related to overprotective, if well intentioned, caring that many girls receive from parents and carers.

It has been noted that many parents allow their sons to take more physical risks than their daughters, and have different views of danger for each gender. There is a high correlation between girls' confidence levels and time spent outdoors. Both genders will experience less fear and presumably greater self-confidence if they were to spend more free time outside, whether in their neighbourhoods or in bush environments.

Develop autonomy

An interesting study of self-critical kids conducted in Singapore found that highly critical kids are likely to have highly intrusive, over-controlling parents. Nearly 80 per cent of perfectionist children had a parent who was intrusive, or highly controlling. I suspect these findings are valid for Australia, where many parents increasingly try to oversee the minutiae of their kids' lives. These include influencing their choice of clothes, food, after-school leisure and even friends. This move to influence and control robs children of the autonomy they need to gain mastery over their own lives, and the confidence and competence that comes with it. And, as this study suggests, it quite possibly also leads to perfectionism and dissatisfaction with performance of any kind. The solution is for parents to step back and help their children to become independent problem-solvers rather than solve their problems for them.

Let them decide

Now, I'm not suggesting that parents allow children to make all decisions that concern them. Clearly parents as wise leaders need to call the shots on how the family life is conducted and health and welfare issues such as appropriate bed and bath times. Some things are not up for negotiation. But there are areas where parents can rightfully hand autonomy to children and say, 'It's your call!' Choice of clothes, how they keep their bedroom, what they eat and who they play with are the types of decisions they can make. Naturally, this is age-related and you do need to have some influence, particularly if you can't enter a bedroom because it's bulging with toys, clothes and sports gear. But so often we fight with kids over issues that parents in large families wouldn't think twice about.

Parent of small family	Parent of large family
'Messy bedroom!'	'What bedroom?'
'Didn't eat his meal!'	'I didn't know he was even at the dinner table.'
'Are those friends the right type?'	'Good to see he has mates!'

There's another sort of autonomy

Autonomy is shown when parents allow children to follow their own interests rather than those preferred by parents. Brett, a competitive sporty dad, thought his ten-year-old daughter needed some toughening up, so he encouraged her to compete in triathlons, which were his passion. His daughter soon became fond of triathlons but not for his reasons. She always completed each event but was usually at the back of the field where the more sociable, less competitive kids could be found. While her dad initially wanted to encourage her competitiveness he conceded that she had her own reasons for taking part, so he didn't push his own motivations onto her.

How to encourage kids to be problem-solvers

When parents solve all children's problems we not only increase their dependency on adults but we teach kids to be afraid of making mistakes and to blame themselves for not being good enough. That's fertile ground for anxiety and depressive illness.

So, how can we raise kids to be courageous problem-solvers rather than self-critical scaredy cats? Here are six practical ideas to get you started.

1. **Turn requests into problems for kids to solve**

    Kids get used to bringing their problems to parents to solve. If you keeping solving them, they'll keep bringing them. *'Mum, my sister is annoying me!' 'Dad, can you ask my teacher to pick me for the team?' 'Hey, I can't find my socks!'* It's tempting if you are in a time-poor family to simply jump in and help kids out. Alternatively, you can take a problem-solving approach, cuing them to resolve their own problems and take responsibility for their concerns. *'What can you do to make her stop annoying you?' 'What's the best approach to take with your teacher?' 'Socks, smocks! Where might they be?'*

2. **Ask good questions to prompt problem-solving**
   A problem-solving approach relies on asking good questions, which can be challenging if you are used to solving your child's problems. The first question when a child brings you a problem should be: *'Can you handle this on your own?'* Next should be, *'What do you want me to do to help you solve the problem?'* These questions are not meant to deter children from coming to you; rather, to encourage and teach them to start working through their own concerns themselves.

3. **Coach them through problems and concerns**
   So, your child feels she was unfairly left out of a school sports team by a teacher and asks you to get involved. The easiest solution may be to meet with the teacher and find out what's going on. You may or may not resolve the problem but in doing so you are teaching a child to become dependent on you. Alternatively, you could coach your child to speak to the teacher herself and find out why she was left out. Obviously, there are times when children need their parents to be advocates for them such as when

they are being bullied, but we need to make the most of the opportunities for children to speak for themselves. Better to help your child find the right words to use and discuss the best way to approach another person when they have problems. These are great skills to take into adulthood.

4. **Prepare kids for problems and contingencies**

You may coach your child to be independent – walk to school, spend some time alone at home (when old enough), catch a train with friends – but does he know what to do in an emergency? What happens if he comes home after school and the house is locked? Who should he go to? Discuss different scenarios with children whenever they enter new or potentially risky situations so that they won't fall apart when things don't go their way. Remember the Boy Scouts motto – be prepared!

5. **Show a little faith**

Sometimes you've got to show faith in children. We can easily trip them up with our negative expectations, such as by saying *'Don't spill it!'* to a child who is carrying a glass filled with water. Of course, your child doesn't want to spill it but you've just conveyed your expectations with that statement. We need to be careful that we don't sabotage children's efforts to be independent problem-solvers with comments such as, *'Now don't stuff it up!' 'You'll be okay . . . won't you?' 'You're not very good at looking after yourself!'*

6. **Applaud mistakes and stuff-ups**

Would a child who accidentally breaks a plate in your family while emptying the dishwasher be met with a

'That's really annoying, you can be clumsy sometimes' response or an 'It doesn't matter, thanks for your help' type of response? Hopefully it won't be the first response, because nothing shuts down a child's natural tendencies to extend themselves quicker than an adult who can't abide mistakes. If you have a low-risk-taking, perfectionist nature, consider throwing a little party rather than making a fuss when they make errors so they can learn that mistakes don't reflect on them personally, and that the sun will still shine even if they break a plate, tell a joke that falls flat or don't get a perfect examination score.

Help others

There's one compelling reason your kids should help at home – competency built up through helping promotes greater confidence in children. In short, confident kids are competent kids. Past experience has taught them that they can be successful. One way to help develop a sense of competency is to give kids opportunities to help out at home. There is no need to overburden children with jobs, but a sensible allocation of chores according to their age and study requirements is not only a great help to you, but fantastic training for them. It also builds accountability and a work ethic, both highly valued characteristics for continuing success.

Chores are character-building, particularly when children are expected to do them consistently. It's tempting to excuse kids from helping when the weather's hot and they've had a hard day at school, or when their after-school schedules become filled with activity or when homework deadlines loom and they feel stressed. My advice is – Don't let kids off the hook like this.

Don't pay kids for helping

One of the most frequently asked questions in my parenting seminars relates to chores – *'Should kids be paid to help around the house?'* My answer never changes: definitely not. If independence is your aim as a parent, kids should do chores. By all means provide them with pocket money, but avoid linking it to chores. Helping out in exchange for money develops in children a notion of *What's in it for me?*, which is a self-centred view of life.

The new strict

Do you fit the bill as a strict parent? The definition of a strict parent has changed over the past decade. In years gone by some parents wore the label like a badge of honour! It signified parents who were willing to stand their ground with their kids, who put boundaries in place and made sure they were adhered to, such as being home on time, or not watching too much TV.

There's now a new definition. A 'strict' parent has become someone who makes children do things for themselves and also insists they help at home. They insist their children put their dirty clothes in the laundry. They insist kids make their own lunches in secondary school, and maybe even wash their own clothes. A 'strict' parent is one who insists kids set the meal table – without giving them a cent in return.

'Strict' now refers to getting kids to help rather than placing restrictions on them as befitted its previous definition.

Many parents tell me that they get funny looks when their children help them with the supermarket shopping. When their kids walk a kilometre home from a sports or leisure activity they are made to feel like neglectful parents.

The new parenting normal is for parents to do a lot for their kids, rather than kids doing things for themselves. Anyone who strays from this new normal and develops real independence can be made to feel guilty . . . because they are strict!

Nobody feels like doing chores, but tackling hard things when you don't feel like it builds character and develops a bit of grit that kids can draw on later when they really have to push against adversity.

The job of parents is to make themselves redundant, not in a relational sense, but in a managerial sense from their kids. There is nothing revolutionary about this idea; it's been the aim of parents since the dawn of time. That means we spend a lot of time teaching kids self-help skills (now known as life skills).

These include teaching young children to tie their shoelaces; helping primary-school kids to ask for what they want from adults; and coaching teenagers to negotiate their way safely on public transport as well as problem-solve relational issues they may have with teachers at school.

These are not the activities of 'strict' parents. Rather they are the activities of parents who understand that one of their key roles is to equip kids to stand on their own two feet in the world outside the family home.

The best place to do this is within the family. And the best time to start developing independence is from a young age, when kids are up for it! Don't wait until your children are eighteen to develop self-help skills. If you introduce self-help then, my bet is they won't think you are strict . . . they'll think you've been a soft touch all along and they'll now battle you all the way.

But that's a story for another day!

In the meantime, if the definition of 'strict' has changed, then I urge you to be strict. Your kids will thank you . . . later on, when you've equipped them with the problem-solving and independence skills needed to negotiate the wider world without you.

Three independence-building skills for parents

Traditionally, parents have always found ways to make skill acquisition easy for kids. The busier we get, though, the more likely we are to neglect this vital part of parenting. Here are three time-honoured ways parents have helped their kids become independent, each with a modern spin on it.

1. Put on the training wheels

Hands up if you had a bike with training wheels when you were a kid. If you are a Baby Boomer, my bet is you kept your hands down. It was sink or swim in those days. You rode when you were ready and you probably experienced lots of falls in the process. If you were born after 1965 you probably learned to ride with training wheels. They kept you upright while you learned the knack of balancing. The training wheels helped you to ride at an earlier age, reducing the number of falls, which meant fewer bumps and bruises.

Using training wheels is a modern version of scaffolding, which is what parents have always done to help children master tricky tasks that they are not quite ready for. Some parents give their children a pre-paid mobile phone, which limits the number of calls they make until they are old enough to pay for the calls themselves. Similarly you can teach primary-school children to eat out by turning an at-home evening meal into a restaurant meal and expecting them to eat with their best manners, while you act as a waiter or waitress. There are many opportunities for parents to build scaffolds – or put training wheels on – to support children while they master new competencies, particularly when developing independence in unfamiliar environments.

2. Create cut-down versions

Most modern sports have developed modified versions of their games allowing children from very young ages to participate. Australian Rules, for instance, has removed tackling, reduced the number of players in a team and made grounds smaller so that boys and girls as young as six can participate. This is a massive change to even thirty years ago when ten-year-olds struggled playing on a full-sized ground with a team of eighteen players and tackling was allowed. It worked for some children who were bigger or more talented but it was chaotic for the majority of young players.

There are countless opportunities for parents to create cut-down versions of activities to bring them into the reach of children. For instance, a cut-down version of making a bed for a three-year-old could be smoothing the doona and arranging teddies and a pillow. As a child gains in competency then you can add some complexity to the bed-making. Similarly, a six-year-old can learn to walk to school on their own by being accompanied halfway by an adult until they feel comfortable and become competent enough to go the full journey on their own. A teenager who begins to go out at night can cut her teeth on sleepovers and other supervised gatherings before going to parties and activities without adult supervision. As a general rule, when a child or young person asks if they can do something new or something that extends their boundaries, a parent who works from an independence-building mindset would put steps in place to assist this independence. And often the easiest step is to create a cut-down version of the real thing to help kids develop the confidence and competence they need.

Creating a cut-down version is also a fantastic strategy to enable anxious, nervous and low-risk-taking kids to gain the skills and confidence needed to overcome their fears and anxieties. Such kids need to face their fears rather than avoid them, otherwise they will always struggle.

If, for example, it's a birthday party that's causing intense worry, use a cut-down version so your child only needs to go for the first hour rather than the whole party. You can scaffold their way to independence by arranging for them to go with a friend beforehand, and stay with them until they feel comfortable moving away. You can also create a cut-down version of a party at home with siblings and rehearse how they can introduce themselves and play with others. This may sound contrived but these types of activities are invaluable for helping anxious kids gain mastery over unfamiliar social situations.

3. Do things together

Teaching and training need to be part of the everyday repertoire of a parent. When we are busy it is often easier to do things ourselves, so this may mean we need to add a little extra time to many of our interactions so we can help children acquire the basic skills of living, whether it is a young child learning to do up his shoelaces or a teenager learning how to fill out her first tax return.

Teaching children and young people new skills works well when you do things together. In fact, it's the way that parents traditionally have passed on many skills and competencies to their children. Here's how it works:

- 'You watch me.'
- 'You help me.'
- 'I'll help you.'
- 'I'll watch you.'

I used this method when I gave my twentysomething daughter a crash course in cooking curries – my specialty – when she stayed over recently. The first night she helped me prepare a number of dishes. We repeated the process the next night except that I helped her as she took charge. The same principle applies with all sorts of activities but it's easiest to explain through cooking. You can teach primary-school kids to cook by asking them to help you. Not only do they see what you are doing but they get their hands dirty as well. Then you can turn the tables where you become their helper with some of the recipes they are familiar with.

Independence – a final word

Independence takes many forms and has many faces. It's easiest to develop in children when they are young. Also, not every child in a family will take to independence as willingly as others. If developing independence is something that you haven't focused on before, don't despair. It's never too late to start. Begin where you feel comfortable – perhaps giving some responsibilities to children or setting small tasks to do at home – rather than make huge changes straightaway. Persist rather than give in when you have resisters; the notion of independence is too important for children's future success.

part two

RAISE
independent kids

We need to help our children develop the tools and attributes that will allow them to be successful, self-reliant and civil when we are not around. That is what independence and autonomy is all about. There are currently some high-profile Australian athletes who may be successful and on the surface self-reliant, but behave in less than civil ways towards others. Success, self-reliance and civility are the types of qualities most Australians admire in young people regardless of their profile. I have identified five tools and attributes to focus on that will help children develop a real, lasting sense of independence. They are: Resilience, Accountability, Integrity, Self-confidence and Emotional intelligence. RAISE is an easy acronym for parents to remember.

In this section I will discuss each of these attributes, outline why they are important to your child's success and show you how to develop each skill or attribute in your kids.

chapter two

Resilience

Helping kids bounce forward

Resilience is a concept that has become a part of the parenting lexicon over the past decade or so in Australia and many other developed countries. It's certainly a concept I've been talking and writing about for over two decades, and its importance can't be understated, particularly if you listen to futurists such as Mark McCrindle. He predicts that the children born in 2010 and beyond will have a minimum of five careers and twenty different employers in their lifetime. Gone is the job for life, replaced by a series of mini-careers, according to McCrindle. He claims we need to get used to being employed for the life of a particular project and then be prepared to look for other projects upon completion. If this scenario is accurate, and I suspect it is because it's happening already, then young people entering the workforce of the future will need personal resilience to handle the ups, downs and disappointments that will come from more flexible working arrangements.

My colleague, psychologist Andrew Fuller, refers to resilience as the ability to bungee jump your way through life. It's a fabulous metaphor that suggests the notion of bouncing back from difficulties and getting back on track with your life when difficulties have been experienced. The research around resilience suggests that with the right support and right set of skills most people do bounce back and get back on track. But there's a cohort who don't merely recover from difficulty – they grow through difficulty, with their lives taking on new or greater meaning. They, in effect, bounce *forward* using a negative event as the impetus for growth and development. And that is what we should want for our children – to continually learn and grow from their experiences whether positive or negative.

Is resilience nature or nurture?

Some kids are resilient by nature – their temperament helps them to be mentally and psychologically tough. You know those kids. They get straight back up after a setback or disappointment. Rejection in the playground doesn't faze them. They are flexible enough to cope with changes such as moving from one school to another. They keep working hard in school even if they don't succeed at first. They have a resilient spirit.

Unfortunately, not every child has such natural resilience. The good news is that most of the research on the subject indicates that resilience can be nurtured and developed, particularly when parents themselves are resilient and actively foster this characteristic in their kids.

Resilient kids share four basic skills: autonomy, problem-solving, optimism and social connection. There are many ways parents can develop these skills in their children, but perhaps the easiest and most accessible way is to allow kids to fully contribute to their family. By developing your child's self-help skills, you will promote independence and resourcefulness in them.

Children's life experiences contribute to their resilience

The seemingly small disappointments that kids experience – not being invited to a party, missing being picked in a sports team, not achieving success in a school project the first time – help them learn to cope with hardship and frustration. Coping with minor development issues such as change, sibling conflict and even failure build up a psychological hardiness that will help them when they face some of life's big challenges in adolescence and beyond.

That means that you, as a parent, need to resist sorting out your children's social problems for them; rather, you need to skill them up to solve their own friendship challenges. Sometimes parents can create problems by interfering in children's disputes. From the resilience perspective you are better off coaching kids through some of their more challenging moments and reviewing what they may have learned for next time.

You also need to put children and young people in situations where they need to draw on their resourcefulness. Camps and adventure activities are great ways for kids to stretch themselves and test their problem-solving and coping skills. My second daughter, Emma (she of the Danish Adventure), believes that a ten-day adventure camp she went on as a fourteen-year-old was the defining event of her early adolescence. It involved real physical endeavour, which stretched her to the limits, literally bringing her to tears on many occasions. It was the first time she realised that she could cope with being separated from her friends and family as well as the comforts of home. While away in Denmark she frequently drew on the coping skills she had learned on her ten-day camp to overcome homesickness and deal with the challenges of living in an unfamiliar environment for such a long time.

Regular positive parent–child interactions help kids pick up the basic social skills needed to interact with their peers, as well as more subtle resilience skills such as humour, goal-setting and persistence. So, parents need to look for as many opportunities as possible to spend time with and talk to their kids.

Kids also learn optimism from home. Martin Seligman, author of *The Optimistic Child*, found that kids pick up the explanatory style of the parent they spend most time around, usually mothers, by the age of eight. If that parent tends to be optimistic, it's likely the child will be too. In other words, a 'can do' attitude pays off.

Promoting resilience in kids is not a single event but a continual process. It requires parents, teachers and other adults to look for opportunities for kids to stretch themselves socially, academically and even emotionally.

Resilience starts with empathy

In my book *Thriving!* I wrote that kids typically face many Hardships, Frustrations and Difficulties (HFDs) as they go through different stages of development. Pets pass away. Friends move town. Families move home and kids change schools. Children miss being picked for a team. Teens are left off party invitation lists. How stressful these everyday events are for them will depend on many factors, including their own spirit, the support they get from home and their coping skills. But the first response of parents when children genuinely come to them with their worries and concerns needs to be an empathetic one.

When your sensitive child comes home from school crying because he thinks everyone is picking on him; or your teenager tells you in a heartfelt way that she wished she looked more like Anita that skinny girl whom everyone loves; or your eight-year-old cries on your shoulder that no matter how hard he tries he just can't get his head around maths at school – the three words they need to hear from you are *'I get it!'* They want to know you genuinely understand what they are going through. They need you to be empathetic (*'me too'*), not sympathetic (*'poor you'*).

Showing empathy is not easy. It means you have to stop what you are doing, listen to what your child is saying and how they are feeling, and take yourself to a time when you felt a similar way. Everyone knows how hurtful cruel and cutting remarks can be. Everyone knows what it's like to look at a colleague or peer and wish that you had the easy ride, the looks or the natural advantages they have. We've all felt the frustration of no matter how hard we tried we just couldn't grasp a skill or concept. But it takes time, effort and the vulnerability to take yourself to a time and space when you've experienced something similar. Such empathetic support is what children need to help them cope with stressful or difficult situations – and this is part of the redundancy parenting philosophy.

Coping with HFDs both big and small is part of growing up. Some kids cope with stressful or difficult situations better than others. They seem to naturally get by. Others need parental input to help them cope with seemingly minor situations. Regardless of the type of child you have, they all benefit from an empathetic

'I understand' response from a parent when they experience difficulties and hardships.

Once you've reached, you can teach

When children experience hardships it is really helpful if parents and teachers can assist them to process what happened to them. Children are faulty observers and often have difficulty seeing the full picture, particularly when they are so close to the situation. Help your child see the full picture and in doing so they may realise that things may not be as bad as they seem. Here are three useful approaches you can take to help kids successfully process difficult events.

1. Keep things in perspective

It's natural when things go wrong to think that life will never be the same again. I recall as a teenager doing poorer than expected in my end of school exams, and missing the tertiary course I had set for myself. At the time it was such a catastrophe. I thought that there was no point taking another course – naturally, I would hate it. Of course, I undertook a teaching course, which I really enjoyed and I didn't look back.

Breaking up with a friend, losing close sports events and being on the receiving end of teasing can at the time seem like events from which we will never recover.

Catastrophising (jumping immediately to the worst possible scenario) only exaggerates kids' worries and makes them feel even more anxious. It always helps to keep your sense of proportion, but it's not easy when emotions run high. We all exaggerate our problems from time to time, particularly when we are under stress. It takes a cool customer to moderate their thinking the whole time, but some kids are prone to jumping to the worst-case scenario, even when the events are quite minor.

If your child is a serial catastrophiser, always seeing the worst case in a negative situation, try to change their thinking so they learn to keep things in perspective. Ask them the following questions to challenge their catastrophic thinking:

- **'What's the most likely scenario?'** Sometimes it's useful to introduce a dose of old-fashioned rational thinking for those kids who always assume the worst will happen to them. 'Yep, you could break your leg if you go skiing. But the odds are that you won't.'
- **'You may be right, but does it *really* matter?'** One way to help hardcore catastrophisers is to admit that they could be right, but then ask them to imagine that the worst possible scenario actually happens. Then challenge them to understand that even the worst possible scenario is not so bad after all. This is the type of reality check many kids need.
- **'Where does this fit on the disaster meter?'** Catastrophisers tie themselves in a knot about relatively insignificant things. Okay, making a fool out of themselves when they give a talk at school may not be insignificant to kids, but there are plenty of worse things that could happen. Help them get some perspective by giving their worry a score out of ten, on how important the issue really is.
- **'Is that helpful thinking?'** Sometimes kids' thinking is so out of whack with reality that they become anxious about minor things. Thinking such as, *'Everyone must like me,' 'I must never make a mistake'* and *'Bad things always happen to me'* are extreme and need to be replaced by more moderate, realistic thoughts, such as, *'It would be nice if everyone liked me but not everyone will. It's important to have some good friends.'*

2. Normalise the situation

It's human nature to think that we are the only ones to experience bad things, but this is rarely the case. Everyone has experienced loss, rejection, disappointment and conflict – it is unlikely that there is a situation so unique that you are the ONLY person to have experienced it. Normalising a situation is an aspect of optimism. When you realise that others also experience similar difficulties and survive you feel more hopeful.

When bad things happen to kids help them to normalise a situation rather than personalise it. *You are not the only one to experience this* is a powerful concept for kids to grasp. Even when they experience extremely distressing events such as family breakdown, help them understand that other families break down too and reassure them that as difficult as it may seem, children learn to cope.

From a mental-health perspective we need to allow children to experience the full gamut of emotions, including sadness, loss, fear and anxiety. These emotions are normal and healthy. Kids need to hear comments such as: *'Everyone feels bad sometimes.' 'It's okay to feel sad or scared. Most people would be in this situation.' 'It's not just you. You are not the first person that this has happened to.'* They also need to be allowed to express their disappointment, frustration and other emotions. They need to have their genuine worries and disappointment validated, but they also benefit from having someone who reminds them that as bad as things may seem right now that *this too shall pass and life will return to normal.*

3. Don't let this spoil everything

Help your child to park their bad thoughts somewhere when they are worried or continually fretting over something unpleasant.

The ability to compartmentalise bad events and keep them from affecting all areas of life is a powerful coping skill that will help them to function normally and then revisit the events when it suits. For instance, if something negative happens at recess at school they can stop it from spoiling their whole day. They can think about something else when they are in class and revisit the issue later on. Sometimes it helps to write down worries and then revisit them at a later date.

This strategy requires kids to distract themselves, think about something else and focus on the job at hand. My mum had two fantastic sayings that she employed to remind me that I shouldn't let one bad event spoil everything. She would often say, *'Park your problems for a while and then come back to them later on.'* I remember that I used to feel relieved when she said this because it gave me permission not to worry. She also often said when something unpleasant had happened, *'Don't let this one thing wreck your whole day.'* Hmm. Easy for her to say!

Seven resilience robbers and what to do instead

Sometimes, despite your best intentions, old parenting habits can actually feed children's fears and anxiety. Check out the following common parenting mistakes that reduce children's resilience.

Robber #1: Fight all their battles for them
There's nothing wrong with going in to bat when kids struggle or meet with difficulty inside or outside school, but make sure this is the last resort, not the first option.
Resilience alternative: Give kids the opportunity to develop their own resourcefulness.

Robber #2: Make their problem, your problem

Sometimes parents take too much responsibility for issues that are really up to children to work out or decide. We put jumpers on them even when they don't feel the cold, remind them to return library books and wake them in the morning when they are capable of getting themselves up.

Resilience alternative: Make their problem, their problem.

Robber #3: Give kids too much voice

In this era of giving children a voice it is easy to go overboard and allow them too much of a say in what happens to them. Kids often take the easy option to avoid hard or unpleasant situations.

Resilience alternative: Make decisions for kids and expect them to adjust and cope.

Robber #4: Put unrealistic or relentless pressure on kids to perform

Expectations about success and achievement are important. Too low and kids will too easily meet them. Too high and kids can give up. Too much and kids can experience anxiety.

Resilience alternative: Keep expectations in line with children's abilities and don't put excessive pressure on them.

Robber #5: Let kids give in too easily

Resilient learners link success with effort. They don't give up because they don't like a teacher or when confronted with complex activities. Similarly they don't bail out of a sporting team halfway through the season because the team is not winning or they are not enjoying it.

Resilience alternative: Encourage kids to complete what they have started even if the results aren't perfect.

Robber #6: Neglect to develop independence

Don't wait until they are teenagers to develop the skills of independent living. Start early and promote a broad skillset so that they can look after themselves if you are not around.

Resilience alternative: Don't routinely do for kids what they can do for themselves.

Robber #7: Rescue kids from challenging or stressful situations

There are many times kids are put in situations outside their comfort zone for a period. For instance, giving a talk, singing at the school concert or going on school camp may be challenges for some kids. They are all situations that kids usually cope with, so show your confidence in them and skill them up rather than opt for avoidance.

Resilience alternative: Teach kids that overcoming challenges enables them to grow and improve.

Sometimes the manageable hardships that children experience such as a friend moving away, not being invited to a party or completing a difficult school project are fabulous learning opportunities. They help kids to stretch and grow, and teach kids that they are capable of coping when they meet some of life's curve balls. And that is a huge lesson to learn at any age.

Encourage persistence

The ability to persist at a task and see it through to the end is one of the most important success attributes that you can develop in a child.

There are numerous times every day when children must persist rather than give in. A four-year-old learning to tie shoelaces must persist. A primary-school student must show determination to finish tasks. A secondary-school student needs to work through difficulties, particularly those he doesn't understand or complete right away. They need to be able to persist when work gets hard or life gets tough.

Some children are more naturally predisposed to persist than others. They have a determined, even competitive, streak in their temperament that doesn't allow them to give in. These children and young people can drive themselves very hard to succeed.

The results of the Australian Temperament Project released in 2001 show that persistence is the one temperamental factor that can be improved over time. Parents and teachers can develop persistence in children and also impede its development by making life too easy so that the children don't have opportunities to just hang in there.

Parents can promote persistence by encouraging their children to keep going and not give in at the slightest hurdle. They can be a sounding board for children's gripes but they should show confidence in their ability to cope and get through their difficulties. 'You can do it' is far more powerful in terms of promoting an attitude of persistence than, 'If it is a little too hard, then try something else.'

Let children know that there is a correlation between effort and success.

Here are four practical strategies you can use to promote a sense of persistence in your children.

1. **Develop a vocabulary for persistence.** Phrases such as *'Hang tough'*, *'Work hard'* and *'Hang in there'* can become part of their everyday vocabulary.
2. **Point out to your children when they stick at a task.** Most parents know it pays off when they catch their children being good but it also pays off to catch them being persistent. Also remind them that persistence generally has its rewards.
3. **Help your children to remember successes.** Let them know that persistence has worked for them before and it will again if they hang in there.
4. **Talk about hard work with your children.** They need to understand that to be successful they need to do things that are not fun or easy.

Develop language around resilience

Families develop their own language that has meaning for them. *'This is non-negotiable'* has significant meaning in my tribe, going well beyond displaying an unwillingness to argue or negotiate. It is a term that found its way into the family lexicon when I was parenting adolescents. It usually accompanied a parent request or expectation. *'You need to come to your grandma's place this Sunday. It's her birthday so it's non-negotiable.'* End of story! No arguments entered into!

This is such a strong part of our family's proprietary language that my adult daughter's husband uses it when establishing the limits of his familial obligations. When testing the waters to see if he's expected at a family function he'll invariably ask, *'Is next Friday night's dinner a non-negotiable?'*

The term has withstood the test of time.

Just as families develop their own language around what's important to them, and around how they function, they develop their own words and phrases to help each other get through the inevitable tough times that each person experiences. The language of resilience generally refers to coping strategies such as empathy, humour and acceptance.

As a rule of thumb, in resilient families children and adults tune in to the needs of each other, choosing situation-specific language, rather than simply regurgitating generalised feel-good or get-on-with-it platitudes.

Following are twelve examples of the language of resilience, the coping skills each reflects and the types of situations where they are applicable.

1. *'Come on, laugh it off.'* **Strategy:** Humour. **Good for:** Kids who experience disappointment, failure and even loss.

   Humour is a great coping strategy and a powerful tool for resilience because it heightens feelings of control. Some children and young people will naturally crack jokes or make fun of seemingly serious situations. This is a fantastic way to release stress and handle feelings of helplessness. As a parent you may need to lighten up tense situations by introducing humour of your own, which is something that many dads do really well.

2. *'Don't let this spoil everything.'* **Strategy:** Containing thinking. **Good for:** Kids who feel overwhelmed; kids who experience rejection; perfectionists.

   The ability to compartmentalise bad events and keep them from affecting all areas of life is a powerful coping skill and one that kids can learn within their family. When something unpleasant happens during recess, for example, kids need to park their thinking about that event so they can get on with the rest of the day.

3. *'Let's take a break.'* **Strategy:** Distraction. **Good for:** Kids experiencing stressful situations; kids who think too much; kids with busy lives.

   When kids are troubled by events, or spend too much time brooding, it helps to do something to get their mind off things for a time. Playing games, spending time together, watching some TV and going out are all good distracters for worried, anxious or stressed kids. Self-distraction is healthy, providing some welcome perspective. It also prevents kids from replaying awful experiences in their head, blowing them out of proportion.

4. *'Who have you spoken to about this?'* **Strategy:** Seeking help. **Good for:** Kids who experience bullying and social problems; handling all types of personal worries.

   Resilient people seek solace in the company of others when they experience difficulty. That's why social connection is such a strong preventative strategy for young people. The promotion of help-seeking behaviours is one of the best coping strategies of all. Even if kids don't overtly talk about what's bothering them, it can be immensely reassuring to spend time around others who are empathetic, understanding and willing to listen and help.

5. *'Everyone feels bad sometimes.'* **Strategy:** Normalising events. **Good for:** Kids who lose perspective; kids who take things too personally; persistent worriers.

   It's human nature to think that we are the only people who have experienced certain situations. However, the human condition suggests that this is rarely the case. Let kids know that they are not alone in their experiences, and just as others have discovered, 'this difficult situation too will pass'. They need to hang in there (another piece of resilience language)!

6. *'I know it looks bad now but you will get through this.'* **Strategy:** Offering hope. **Good for:** Kids experiencing loss, bullying, change or extreme disappointment.

   There are times when parents can do nothing else but keep their child's chin up and encourage them when life doesn't go their way. Being the hopeful person can be hard work, that's why parents need to be supported by resilient people and workplaces too. It helps to be mindful that a child or young person's resilience is nurtured by the presence of at least one supportive adult. You may have to be that person!

7. *'What can you learn from this so it doesn't happen next time?'* **Strategy:** Positive reframing. **Good for:** Kids who make mistakes, let others down or experience personal disappointment.

   One of the common attributes of optimistic people is their ability to find a learning opportunity, or look for a message, in difficult or negative situations. Parents can help kids reframe events to help them see things differently. For instance, rather than regard a public speaking opportunity as problematic and a chance to look foolish, it's better to reframe it as a challenge and a chance to shine. It also helps when parents model reframing so kids see you changing how you view seemingly negative or worrying situations.

8. *'You didn't make this happen.'* **Strategy:** Realistic attribution (blame fairly). **Good for:** Kids who blame themselves, take things too personally.

   Self-blame is one of the enemies of resilience. Kids who blame themselves for negative events often think irrationally and can experience loss of hope. Parents can help kids see that most things that happen, whether good or bad, occur due to a mixture of luck, other people's actions and their own actions. Any sportsman who has missed the winning goal or dropped an important catch needs to be reminded that luck and other people's inaction were also a factor in their team not getting over the line.

9. *'Don't worry – relax and see what happens!'* **Strategy:** Acceptance. **Good for:** Kids who worry about exams or performing poorly in any endeavour; pessimists.

   If you've ever been driving to an important event only to be stuck in traffic, you know that there are some situations you just can't control. The only way to cope is to accept what's happening, because worrying and fretting won't get you anywhere. Similarly, parents with a resilience mindset can help kids understand what's worth worrying about and what's not; and also that some things won't change no matter how much kids fret or beat themselves up!

10. *'This isn't the end of the world.'* **Strategy:** Maintaining perspective. **Good for:** Kids who exaggerate their worries or blow things out of proportion.

    While most of us catastrophise by exaggerating our worries at times, jumping to the worst possible scenario is a habit that only exaggerates anxiety. When kids constantly think this way, challenge their views. *'Yes, you could end up not knowing anyone at camp but you won't be the only one. Besides, you'll probably end up making new friends like you generally do.'*

11. *'You could be right. But have you thought about . . .'* **Strategy:** Flexible thinking. **Good for:** Kids who catastrophise; kids who experience extreme feelings; kids who exaggerate.

    Many children and young people talk in extremes – 'awesome', 'the best', 'the worst' and 'gross' roll off their tongues easily.

Unfortunately, their extreme language leads to extreme emotional responses. Develop the habit of winding back their language by introducing shades of grey, rather than black and white. Replace *'I'm furious!'* with *'I'm annoyed.'* *'It's an absolute disaster!'* with *'It's a pain.'* *'I can't stand it!'* with *'I don't like it.'* Realistic language leads to realistic thinking, which helps kids handle many ordinary situations that they have blown out of proportion.

12. *'What can we do about this?'* **Strategy:** Taking action. **Good for:** Kids who mope; kids who experience disappointment; kids who feel inadequate.

Kids can sometimes feel overwhelmed by events such as constant failure, constant rejection or always narrowly missing being picked for a team. They can be overwhelmed by feelings of inadequacy and helplessness. Action is often the best remedy. Help them take the first step forward. Set some goals. Make some plans. Identify the first step and hold their hand while they take it.

Time alone for resilience

Close your eyes and say the word 'alone' to yourself. Does it have a positive or negative connotation? I'd suggest negative because it's close to 'lonely', and loneliness is a state we all want to avoid. I can't help but think of *Home Alone*, that film about a young boy who spends Christmas on his own after he is accidentally left behind when his family goes on holiday.

But time spent alone is good. Kids need to have opportunities to spend time alone every day. It helps them feel comfortable in their own skin. It also gives them a chance to reflect on the day's activities and process the good and the bad.

Interestingly, only-children always do better on average in well-being and achievement tests than children with siblings. On the achievement side this makes sense because only-children spend more time exposed to adult thinking, language and concepts. I suspect from a resilience perspective only-children have plenty of advantages because they spend more time alone, in their own company, than children who have siblings. Most only-children I know really like themselves. In terms of self-esteem and well-being, they seem to be ahead of many of their counterparts who spend less time alone.

Although I had siblings, due to a large gap in ages I was virtually raised as an only child. I remember that as a primary-school child I used to retreat to my bedroom and spend a lot of time alone. I loved it. Looking back I used to process my day when I was alone. I also used to let my imagination run wild, which was both fun and scary. But I also think it gave me a chance to be comfortable with who I was. That's important for resilience because, let's face it, you've got to like yourself if you are going to thrive.

Like most of these things it is all about balance. In my case I also spent a lot of time with siblings and friends. However, in the current non-stop world it can be hard sometimes for kids to find time to be alone, so you may need to make a more conscious effort to help your kids find that space.

It's important that they do.

Resilience – a final word

Perhaps the easiest way to avoid spoonfeeding your kids is to develop a mindset for resilience. That means being on the lookout for developing your child's coping abilities; being willing to remember your own struggles and difficulties that mirror those of your child; and being the hopeful person who keeps your child's chin up when they experience difficulties that seem as if they just won't go away. Things *will* get better. They always do. That's a fabulous resilience lesson to learn.

chapter three

Accountability

Be accountable for your actions

Kids aren't ready for self-reliance until they are able to fit into the many groups they will come into contact with as adults. That means that parents continually need to develop a sense of 'other' in their children. This job starts when children are very young – toddlers, in fact. Their first group is their family, so they need to learn to negotiate the many and varied situations that arise in their home. Keeping toddlers safe means keeping them away from dangerous objects, keeping them contained and keeping an eye on their whereabouts. Making them social is about having them fit into the family schedule, while ensuring that their needs are met. Helping them be people-smart means exposing them to various social situations involving others, including playing alongside other children.

Children's horizons expand with age, so our job of socialising kids is a continuous process. Socially smart kids don't operate in a bubble. They know that their behaviour impacts others, so they are mindful of the thoughts, feelings and behaviours of others. This mindfulness is age-related. It's generally hard work during the preschool years, becomes easier during primary school and can again be difficult with teenagers whose behaviour and consideration for others frequently regresses, or waxes and wanes.

Arrested social development

Recently I was waiting in the luggage queue at an airport as two teenaged girls wrestled with each other, continually knocking me in the back and disturbing my luggage next to me. I glared at them on a number of occasions but the girls seemed aware of my discomfort and continued their friendly fire without apology. At first I put this down to thoughtless teenage behaviour, but I then saw their parents, who were standing next to them and had made no attempt to pull them into line. This was more than typical teenage thoughtless behaviour. They were either not aware of the rights of others, or they chose to ignore reasonable standards of behaviour. Either way I suspect these girls will be limited in their ability to move within the many and varied social groups that they will encounter in their expanding social world.

Middle adolescents, those in the fourteen- to sixteen-year age group, famously adopt the same persona for all their social groups. So, they'll speak to their teachers, their parents, their wider family using the same language and tone of voice that they'd use when interacting with their peers. In the meantime parents are frantically reminding their young people to speak properly much in the same way as they reminded toddlers to look adults in the eye and say thank you. Teenagers generally grow out of that around the end of their secondary schooling if they've been taught to consider the rights of others. These lessons enable children and young people to flexibly and successfully move in and out of the many different groups in their lives. This social flexibility enables them to enjoy a variety of relationships across different generations, social strata and cultures. Inevitably, children and young people who are raised without giving due consideration to the many and varied social situations and groups they encounter when growing up, much like the teenagers at the airport, won't have the same access to a wide range of social groups as those with the necessary social flexibility. Arrested social development that comes with an egocentric view of the world has its price.

Here's a handy definition of accountable behaviour

If it's a parent's job to socialise kids, then it helps to have a definition for behaviour. This simple definition is applicable for all age groups and situations. In any situation ask yourself: What does this social situation reasonably require of my child at their age and stage of development?

If you are sitting at the dinner table, it's a reasonable expectation that children eat their meal and also socialise. How much they eat and how social they are will depend on many variables. However, the situation is pretty clear, indicated by either a rule (*'We sit down while we eat at the table'*) or an expectation (*'You know we normally sit down at the table while we eat'*). Behaviour that fits outside those norms – fighting, throwing food or making inappropriate noise – can be considered poor behaviour because it's not what the situation expects. These are social situations, so children need to be mindful of the needs and rights of others, including parents.

Accountability is developmental

Children in the first few years of life are hard work for any parent. Parents today are poorly prepared compared to their predecessors for just how big a struggle children of this age can pose. This age group experiences massive physical development that is not matched by the same rate of intellectual maturation. Children around the age of one and a half to two and a half are like international airports – there is a huge amount of activity that is governed by very small control towers. Currently, children in the two- to three-year age group present the most challenges to parents behaviourally, with the eleven- to fourteen-year age group a close second. It is not surprising that these two ages present most difficulty to parents, because both are significant transition stages where the pursuit of independence is paramount.

While society has changed significantly over the past few decades, children and their developmental needs haven't altered much. Children develop best in a stable environment where they feel that they are valued, loved and listened to. They prefer an orderly environment to a chaotic one, and they need someone within that environment to help them learn to be safe and sociable as they grow and develop. That role is one that loving parents can fill. Many parents feel decidedly uncomfortable with this type of teaching role. Once referred to as discipline, now many parents feel uncomfortable with this term. They shouldn't, though, because the word derives from a Latin word meaning 'to teach', which is essentially what teachers and carers do to help kids stay safe and to fit in to their various groups, including their family.

The accountability framework

Kids don't behave in a bubble. Their behaviour generally has a social impact. The nature of social groups means that we are constantly adjusting our behaviours to suit the needs and rights of others. That way we can live together. This principle applies just as much to kids as it does to adults, but kids need adult assistance to teach them how to behave well. It helps to be mindful of the relationship between rights, rules and responsibilities when teaching our kids to become social. Parents who use this as a frame of reference are less likely to raise children and young people with an enlarged sense of entitlement who behave selfishly and obnoxiously around others, particularly in public. Here's how it works.

Children, like adults, have social rights that are granted by others. Mr 3 has a right to play with his toys in the living room. Miss 7 has a right to join her family at the dinner table. Mr 15 has a right to go out in the evening with friends. With these rights go responsibilities.

Mr 3's right to play with his toys in the living room comes with a responsibility to pack the toys away at an agreed time such as the end of the day. Miss 7 has a responsibility to eat her meal relatively quietly without disturbing others; noisy arguments and food fights may be fun for her but they disturb the rights of others – namely parents. Mr 15's right to go out with friends at night is accompanied by a responsibility to come home on time, keep his parents informed about his movements and other agreed behaviours. A failure to comply with these expectations or agreed behaviours means that the rights can be removed temporarily, or until kids show that they can be responsible enough to comply. Frequently, rules (also known as limits and boundaries) are put in place to help kids behave responsibly. Kids will push against boundaries with pestering, whining, tantrums and other ways to show their displeasure about a third of the time, which can make discipline, or teaching kids to behave responsibly, hard work. In Part 3 I will discuss the notion of managing like a cat, which makes teaching and managing children's behaviour easier and more effective for parents.

Use behavioural consequences to promote accountability

The use of behavioural consequences is a way of teaching children to take greater responsibility for their lives and to learn to make smarter choices. There are two types of consequences – logical and natural.

A *logical consequence* is used more frequently in family situations. It requires adult intervention and is used when behaviour disturbs other people. A child who makes a noise in the family room is asked to leave; children who fight in the family room lose the right to watch television there; and children who refuse to tidy their toys lose them for a period of time.

Logical consequences are effective for children who resent parental meddling in their affairs, because children clearly relate misbehaviour with its outcome.

Logical consequences usually involve, either:

a) Withdrawal of a right or access to a person, a place or possessions – e.g. lose the right to go out if home later than agreed; toys temporarily lost if not put away; leave the meal table if fighting; or

b) Making amends – make up in some way for unfair treatment of another or for the loss or breakage of a possession, such as payment, part payment of or fixing something broken, or an apology for hurting someone.

A *natural consequence* involves virtually no adult interference. A child who leaves a raincoat at home will get wet; a child who spends all his pocket money on the first day will have nothing for the weekend; and a child who oversleeps and misses the bus must walk to school. In these examples children learn from the direct consequences of their own decisions and thus they are not protected from negative outcomes from their parents. It can safely be said that experiencing the natural consequences of poor choices can be the toughest lessons of all to heed, so it takes strong parents to resist stepping in to rescue kids.

I recall a time when my then fifteen-year-old son packed his week's supply of food for an outdoor-adventure school camp. Despite frequent parental reminders and wise guidance he paid scant regard to his rations. So, he took a week's supply of pasta to cover all evening meals. Experience was a great teacher. After three nights of pasta with little flavouring he realised the folly of his choice; the following year he made sure he took a varied menu to camp. My son, like many boys, is a heuristic learner – he learns from experience rather than by listening to the advice of others. If we want kids to make better choices in the future they need to experience the consequences of their poor choices rather than be protected or rescued from discomfort or mistakes. If not, we rob them of prime learning opportunities and they'll always be reliant on others, including parents, to get them out of scrapes.

Reward responsible behaviour with greater freedom

The flip side of the rights, rules and responsibilities framework is that we can reward responsible behaviour by extending children's rights. It can be difficult to know when we should push boundaries and limits out for kids in any area whether it's technology use, suitable bed-times or even moving around the neighbourhood. My suggestion is to be a little more restrictive at first, so you are able to grant children and young people more freedom as a reward for their responsible behaviour.

Relationship restoration

Problem-ownership promotes responsibility and is a mark of maturity. Sometimes we take responsibility away from kids by solving their problems for them. We do this when we cover for them when they can't get their homework in on time; or give them extra pocket money when they spend it too quickly; or do their chores for them when they forget.

We can all cite examples where we resolved kids' problems for them. Guilty, your honour! I've done it far too often myself.

Sibling relationships

One area of problem-ownership that is easily overlooked is sibling relationships. As every parent of two or more children knows, siblings can say and do awful things to each other. Tween and teen girls with their more advanced intimacy skills compared to boys can be particularly venomous and nasty to each other. They know what upsets others and will reveal secrets and confidences in ways that can be cutting. Boys are more likely to use physical means to quickly resolve conflict in their favour. Either way, relationships can be fractured and need to be repaired.

Jeffrey Kluger in his book *The Sibling Effect* maintains that when left to their own devices siblings will resolve their differences far more quickly than when parents interfere. However, as Kluger notes, there are some children who will wait until hell freezes over before they'll repair a relationship with a sibling.

I can recall numerous times when one of my children was given the cold shoulder by a sibling because of something they had said or done. The shunned child would invariably ask me to sort out the problem, wanting me to get their sibling to talk to them, or in child-speak, *'Stop him/her being mean to me!'*

In this situation I tried to act like Switzerland – remain neutral in times of conflict. However, I did give them ideas about how they could fix the situation with their upset sibling.

If you experience similar challenges with your children, here are three responses you can make, that shift the problem to where it actually lies.

'How can you fix this?'

'How can you make it up to your sister/brother?'

'Have you asked your sister/brother to forgive you?'

Relationship restoration is a lifelong skill. It can involve all or some of the following: swallowing your pride, asking for forgiveness, making up, giving something back, not holding a grudge and moving on.

Relationship restoration between siblings is not something parents can do. We can, though, encourage kids to own their relationships, face up to any issues and make amends for any wrong doing. Relationship restoration also develops empathy in kids, which everyone knows is a powerful relationship skill.

It also helps if kids see their parents restoring relationships without guilt or manipulation and making amends in a giving, mature way.

Accountability – a final word

Real independence is always partnered with accountability. When kids don't hold themselves accountable they are reliant on others to excuse them or rescue them. Allowing kids to become accountable and take responsibility for their choices can make a loving parent feel decidedly bad at times. After all, it can be difficult to watch your kids struggle, or even to stand back and allow them to experience natural consequences. But encouraging kids to become accountable for their actions and behaviours is one of the most important jobs of any parent. It always has been, and always should be. It's just the methodology – how we make accountability happen – that changes over time.

chapter four

Integrity

'Do what's right. Not what's easy.' I heard my wife Sue say this to our children often when a social circumstance presented them with a moral dilemma. Times such as when they agreed to visit a friend's house only to get a better offer elsewhere; when they'd hurt a sibling's feelings and they took the easy option of staying out of their way rather than approaching them to make an apology; and when they'd tell a small lie to excuse themselves from a party or school event that they were expected to attend.

'Do what's right' is an integrity statement. In many ways it's a moral declaration – a declaration of character. Every parent wants to raise kids to be fine young people. But to do this we need to instil in kids more than just skills, attitudes and positive behaviours. We need to provide a compass to help them navigate the myriad of decisions they make every day as children and as teenagers. Integrity sits at the top of that compass. Integrity is the rock star of character; many other traits and characteristics – including respect, responsibility, honesty and fairness – begin when you act with integrity.

A sense of integrity is important for a child's independence because it's the basis of reasoned and socially focused self-control and self-management. The job of parents is to move their children from 'Me' to 'We'. 'Me' is a very self-centred place where kids believe the world revolves around them and is there to meet their needs. 'We' is an other-centred place where kids learn to fit into the many different groups that they belong to, including their family, class and friendship groups. 'We' requires a child to compromise when his needs collide with those of others; it requires a child to consider how his words and actions impact others; and it requires a child to share his time and space with others. Integrity is the great socialising agent for a child. They may get by without courage, endurance and grit but they won't get far socially without integrity.

How kids develop integrity

Integrity, like other aspects of character, is developed through a complex mix of temperament, cultural expectations and nurture, but a parent's role is central to its development. Generally, children first witness integrity in action close up through their parents and siblings' behaviours at home. It's also at home that children experience the disciplinary framework that makes it easier for them to 'do the right thing'. It's within the context of a family that a child first experiences the expectations that he should consider others when he behaves. 'Jai, come to the meal table now, we're all waiting,' is a statement of socialisation. What remains unspoken is, 'Please stop what you are doing and think of others. We are thinking about you, so we're not eating until *you join us.'* It's through the myriad of small interactions we have with children on a daily basis that integrity is promoted and developed.

Children wear L plates when it comes to developing character traits such as integrity. They will often slip up. A child may tell a fib because it's easier than disappointing a parent or facing up to something unpleasant. He will say nasty things about a sibling because he hasn't sufficiently developed the skills to manage his emotions or the reasoning to think things through. He will follow the actions of a friend even though he knows it's not right but he may not know how to say no, making him vulnerable to peer pressure. The world can be a complicated place with many confusing rules and competing expectations. Children need time and parental patience to develop the integrity to make the right choices.

In my book *Thriving!* I wrote how parents can develop a strong family brand that reflects common values and traits. For instance, if all the children in a family have a high work ethic, it's more than likely that hard work is something their parents consciously focus on; it is part of their parents' value system. They have probably developed a vocabulary around hard work, persistence and application (*'You've got to apply yourself'*, *'It takes work but you'll get there in the end'*, *'Time to put your nose to the grindstone'*). They more than likely model hard work so their children see firsthand what hard work looks like, and they probably reward their children for their work ethic either through recognition – *'You deserve to be successful because you have worked so hard'* – or by giving incentives for application – *'If you work hard this term to improve your spelling I'll reward you with something special.'*

Following are five practical ideas to help you place integrity into your family frame.

1. Walk the walk

Children learn to become social by mimicking the behaviours around them. Recently, at a friend's place I saw mimicry in action. After spending some time in conversation, her eight-year-old daughter invited me to jump on the family trampoline – and then she laid out the trampoline rules: 'Take off your shoes. Leave them on the step. You're not allowed to jump when anyone else is on it. You need to take it in turns!' I did a double take; it could have been her mother talking. She used the same tone of voice, the same body language, even the same gestures that her mother uses when she gives instructions to her kids.

No doubt you've experienced this type of mimicry as a parent. The trick is to model the types of behaviours and values, including integrity, that you want to develop in kids. They've a built-in radar for fairness and dishonesty. Berate a child for being dishonest and you'd better make sure you are open and trans-parent in your dealings with others – they can detect hypocrisy a mile away. 'But *you* don't always tell the truth. I heard you phone in to work sick the other day when you wanted to take a day off to play golf!'

Modelling works on two levels. On one level our behaviour shows kids how they should behave in difficult circumstances. And our behaviour also gives kids permission to act in a certain way. Importantly, when we treat others with respect and kindness, make hard moral calls and admit to our mistakes without putting ourselves down we not only show our kids that integrity is impor-tant but we give them permission to act with integrity. It's a matter of, *If Mum can do it, then I can too!*

2. Talk the talk

Families develop their own proprietary language around the behaviours and attributes that are valued. We have a saying in our family that has strong meaning because it was used often – *'This too will pass!'* It's a statement of hope that we used to remind each other that the tough times don't always last. It also reflects a belief that you *will* get through your difficulty and come out the other side. Shared experiences add layers of meanings for everyone in the family.

Similarly, you can build your own family's language around integrity and related values such as honesty, respect, trust, responsibility and fairness. Take the time to reflect on common statements you already use that reflect each of these integrity values. Write them down. Develop them into repeatable phrases – such as *'Honesty is always the best policy!'* – to make them memorable. Predominant family values are always reflected by the language shared by all members. Integrity is taught through action, but reinforced by language.

3. Teach manners

Children up to the age of seven or eight are generally concrete thinkers. That is, they respond to practical, concrete ideas rather than to abstract concepts. It's important, then, to introduce abstract concepts such as integrity in concrete ways to younger children. Perhaps the best way to do this is to insist children use manners. Manners such as saying 'please', 'thank you' and learning to wait their turn in a conversation are social conventions that teach respectful behaviour and generally ensure that the rights of others in a group are protected. Putting manners into practice requires impulse control as well as the ability to hide your feelings at times rather than act on them. In effect, good manners are integrity in action.

4. Use the right discipline approaches

Do you do deals with your kids to encourage them to behave well? Do you offer bribes such as: *'You can stay up for half an hour longer if you are good'*; *'You can use my iPad for five minutes if you eat all your meal'*; *'Clean up your room and I'll give you a treat'*? Bribes and incentives may work in terms of getting cooperation from your tribe but they don't develop children's integrity. The offer of a bribe or a deal teaches a child or young person to think, *What's in this for ME if I behave well?* rather than to think in terms of what's best for others. Offering bribes is also an easy option for parents who want to avoid conflict or the explanations that accompany the expectation of kids 'doing the right thing by others'.

Consequence-based discipline, where kids experience the negative outcomes of their poor decisions and behaviour, is an appropriate approach that promotes real integrity because it encourages them to do what the social situation requires rather than behave well to receive a gift or reward. Consequences work well when they are fair and reasonable. A child who comes home later than agreed from a friend's house may have his right to go out removed for a day or two. That's probably fair and reasonable. But being grounded for a month is unreasonable, unfair as well as unworkable. Consequences are also effective when adults apply them respectfully, maintaining a child's dignity and integrity at the same time. Consequences implicitly promote social behaviours because their use encourages kids to act with integrity. Also, consequences properly applied require that adults act with real integrity as well.

5. Encourage assertiveness, not compliance

Acting with integrity is not always easy for a child or young person, particularly if it means they are swimming against the tide of popular opinion in a peer group. It helps for parents to teach kids how to say no and encourage them to stand up for themselves. Assertiveness begins at home when we allow our kids to voice their concerns in reasonable, respectful ways. It's also important that teenagers learn to articulate their views within the safe confines of their family so that when they are with their peers they have the confidence and wherewithal to voice their concerns about a whole range of behaviours and issues when peers pressure them to comply. Thus the assertiveness needed to act with integrity is generally learned and practised at home.

Integrity – a final word

Every parent wants their child to have the strength and fortitude to do the right thing and not follow the crowd. This is easier for young children because the pull of the group and the allure of the media doesn't have such a strong hold as it so often does in adolescence. Strong-willed children and those who like to have their own way can also find doing the right thing less of a struggle. But the development of integrity and related traits such as respect, honesty and fairness is an important part of a child's moral compass that will help him make smart decisions when you're not around. Generally, integrity is developed in childhood and put to the test in adolescence.

At the time of writing, there are a number of examples of high-profile sportsmen in this country who fail the integrity test very badly. When the pressure is on they behave like children – their integrity deserts them. I suspect it's more that integrity wasn't a character trait that was highly valued by their parents, teachers and early sports coaches. Perhaps their prodigious sporting talent meant that they got everything their own way when growing up and little was expected of them in return. If so, these talented yet spoonfed kids have grown into selfish, difficult-to-admire public figures.

chapter five

Self-confidence

Overcoming fears and anxieties

Lack of self-confidence holds more kids back from reaching their full potential than just about any other issue, including family dysfunction, socio-economic factors and school-funding issues that routinely make headlines. Speak to any teacher and they'll tell you that many of the children in their care are risk-averse, in terms of stepping out of their comfort zone and extending themselves or trying new experiences. This aversion to learning and social risks comes at a time when anxiety is rife among Australian children and young people. A recent study from UNSW and Beyond Blue stated that one in six young Australians suffer from an anxiety condition, and as many as 45 per cent of Year 12 students reported high levels of anxiety.

Anxiety and lack of self-confidence are not mutually exclusive. It's natural for children and young people to feel anxious before some events, such as sitting a test at school, entering a new social situation or performing in a play or concert. Anxiety often associated with nerves or butterflies in the stomach usually helps kids perform at their best. It primes them to perform well. However, it seems we are seeing a new type of anxiety that is debilitating for many children and young people because it leads to avoidance and also impacts mental health and wellbeing. It seems that many kids succumb to rather than conquer their fears and worries, which further impacts their confidence. One way to help kids overcome anxiety is to not only increase their confidence levels but teach them the skills of confidence-building.

Confidence-building is a life skill that few of us were taught. That's one of the reasons many parents struggle when it comes to promoting a real sense of self-esteem in their own children. We've relied too long on a Pollyanna-ish high-praise approach that has failed miserably in raising a generation of children and young people with the real confidence to take learning and social risks. Confidence is both a feeling and, importantly, a skill that when learned can be applied to a variety of situations. We want to put into kids' hands the tools they need to be able to impact their own confidence levels, not only during childhood and adolescence but in their lives as young adults.

Confidence levels change over time

Confidence waxes and wanes, particularly through different stages of development. Toddlers see themselves through their parents' eyes, and they often reflect the confidence levels of their primary parent. Parents at this stage need to make kids feel special and loved. Tell kids that you love them, and avoid giving negative messages and attaching negative labels to kids. This gets tricky because, behaviourally, kids can be challenging for parents. You need to manage their behaviour without dampening their spirit or harming their self-esteem.

In early childhood children are already beginning to separate themselves physically and emotionally from their parents. They start to form a picture of themselves as separate from their parents. They learn about themselves in fairly physical ways, and will begin to compare themselves to others. Parents need to mirror back to children in this age group that they are capable, while also offering a safe, secure and stable environment for them to explore and develop their capabilities.

Children in this age group generally respond strongly to praise. They often have difficulty distinguishing between *what they do* and *who they are*, so when you praise their efforts or performance, they see you praising them. Their self-esteem is linked to how you feel about their behaviours. Consequently, kids in this stage often prefer praise over encouragement. They will usually respond very well to 'descriptive praise' that tells them about their behaviour. *'You packed your toys up straight-away after you finished with them. I love the way you keep your toys tidy.'*

The primary-school years are the prime confidence-building years and the ideal time to teach kids the skills of confidence-building. Some children's confidence levels fall when they start school as they encounter new situations and have new children to meet and new rules to learn. Many children during this stage avoid taking social and learning risks. However, confidence comes from overcoming fears and being brave. Children during this stage benefit from having at least one parent who can really encourage them to take risks, meet new challenges and not be held back by self-doubt and fear.

Children during this stage can often meet with discouragement and disparaging comments from their peers. The best antidote to this is an encouraging, affirming parent.

Confidence levels during adolescence generally fluctuate a great deal. Confidence and self-esteem are linked to many factors including hormonal changes, how a young teenager thinks they look, how successful they feel, and how accepted they are by their peers and family. Young adolescents start to specialise in those areas where they experience success, and cease activities where they can't succeed or only achieve low status in the eyes of their peers. Loving, supportive family relationships can help insulate children in this age group against uncertainty, self-doubt and adverse peer relationships.

Birth order impacts confidence levels

First-born boys are frequently low-risk-takers and can be very self-conscious when young. Eldest girls, on the other hand, often have high levels of confidence, particularly in social settings. Eldest children are also more likely to be perfectionists, many avoiding doing any activity that they can't master straightaway. Youngest children sometimes lack confidence when they are small, yet can become risk-taking, high-achieving teens as their older siblings leave the nest. Many youngest kids are risk-takers because they are not as concerned as their older siblings about the approval of their parents.

Gender impacts confidence levels

When it comes to fears, girls tend to win hands down, having a longer list of things to fear than boys, including spiders, the dark, strangers and new places. It helps, then, to get girls outside at a young age to build up their confidence levels, just as confidence levels are boosted when young girls participate in rough and tumble play with their father. Boys, on the other hand, are more likely than girls to fear failure, which makes confidence-building a big issue when it comes to taking risks as learners.

Confidence is situational and transferrable

Just like adults, kids can be chockfull of confidence facing one situation (such as when they are on a sports field) but be nervous nellies in another (such as in a social setting). Levels of experience, natural skill levels, even individual preferences mean that we naturally approach some events and incidences with greater confidence and assurance than others. It's important, then, that we allow our children and young people to spend time in environments where they can shine. If your child loves the great outdoors and feels comfortable and confident in that environment, it's important to provide plenty of opportunities for them to be outside. Feelings of confidence are transferrable to other areas, particularly when children experience success.

The HEAD–HEART–HANDS approach

Helping children and young people experience greater levels of confidence requires a more complex approach than purely making them feel good about themselves. The 'feel good' movement that has grown over the past few decades – where every competitor in a race gets a ribbon; where praise is scattered like confetti whenever children are around; and where every child in a game of pass the parcel gets a prize – has failed children miserably, producing a generation of young people who are criticism-averse, feel a false sense of entitlement and who still look to their parents to solve many of their problems well into their twenties. It has failed because true confidence comes from the knowledge that you can overcome hardships and work your way through adversity and difficulty, whether social, physical or a learning or work challenge. It's for these reasons that confidence-building is best tackled using the three prime modalities that can either hold kids back or move them forward – their thinking, their feelings and their actions. This head–heart–hands approach tackles confidence-building using all three modalities, importantly putting the tools in kids' hands so they can overcome their fears and anxieties and take more learning risks themselves rather than be dependent on others to make them feel better about themselves. The strategies we shall explore all enhance children's self-sufficiency, independence and resilience.

It's all in their HEAD

A child's confidence levels are influenced by how he views a situation.

For instance, one child may avoid speaking in public, while another will love it. The fact that the same event can bring about two vastly different responses is attributed to the way kids think about these events.

Teaching kids their ABCs

You *can* teach your children new ways to think and influence how they feel and ultimately how they behave by teaching them their ABCs. **A** stands for the activating event, **B** stands for a person's belief about the event and **C** stands for the consequences of your beliefs about an event – namely, how you feel or how you act.

To change **C**, the consequences or reactions to event **A**, it is necessary to change **B**, the beliefs about the event.

If a child were to join a new group or activity, his feelings and behaviour would be determined by his beliefs. If the child thinks that it is too difficult and that no one will like him, then he may feel apprehensive or scared. He may procrastinate about joining the new activity or avoid it altogether. If, however, the child believes that joining in new events is easy he will more than likely be enthusiastic and participate fully. The beliefs a child has may come from past experience of success or failure. More often than not children develop habitual thinking responses to events or activities that are similar to each other. In short, some children have developed a series of positive thinking responses to events, while others have developed negative responses or mindsets. The good news is that these negative mindsets can be changed.

Changing kids' thinking

So, how can you change children's thoughts about an event, situation or person when they are unhelpful? How do you impact thinking that leads to feelings of anxiousness, fear and avoidance? 'Change their thinking' comes off the tongue of a well-meaning parenting educator easily but impacting thinking is a challenge when your eight-year-old is so nervous about performing in a concert that she's about to throw up; or your four-year-old is so scared of the dark that he won't go into his bedroom alone at night; or your teenager hates school so much that she simply refuses to go. Each situation requires a number of different strategies, including: altering their thinking over the long term; plenty of gentle and in some cases insistent encouragement; as well as plenty of old-fashioned hand-holding and scaffolding to help them overcome their fears and anxieties. But there are three fantastic strategies that should be in every parents' toolkit: positive reappraisal, positive self-talk and positive reframing.

1. Positive reappraisal

This is essentially about changing the storyline of a situation. We tend to see situations or events from a narrow view – our own. For instance, when a car cuts in on you on a freeway, you might immediately think that it was done on purpose, then there's a good chance that you'll feel either anger or fear. By looking at it from another viewpoint – such as the driver of the offending car was just careless, he didn't even look – then your reaction will probably shift away from anger or fear to annoyance, which is a less intense emotion. Change the storyline and you change your emotional response.

2. Positive self-talk

Changing the chatter in your brain from something negative, catastrophic or unhelpful to something more realistic, positive and helpful can help you get through a challenging situation. Positive self-talk examples include: *'Stuff happens. I can cope.'* 'It's no big deal.' 'I've put up with worse than someone cutting in on me while I'm driving.'

3. Positive reframing

This is very similar to positive self-talk – in fact, some experts see them as the same thing. But positive reframing is about flipping your thinking by taking a completely opposite view of a situation so you see a different outcome. For instance, a parent who sees their child's difficult behaviour as a problem can flip this by seeing it as a challenge. They can flip a child's stubbornness to knowing his own mind. *'I'll make a fool of myself with my speech,'* can be flipped to *'I'll be able to impress others with my speech.'*

Getting to the HEART of the matter

The debate has been raging for years – should kids receive more praise or more encouragement? I don't think it's an either/or issue. Kids need to receive both from parents, teachers and other trusted adults. The age of your child and the situation they find themselves in play their part.

In the past few decades parents in countries such as Australia, England and the United States have enthusiastically followed the positive-parenting path, constantly showering children with praise. But for some, giving praise for a job well done has become like a nervous tic.

'You finished your meal. What a guy!'

'That's the best work I've ever seen!'

'You are such a clever little swimming girl.'

'You used the toilet. Let's ring Grandma and tell her what a clever girl you are!'

Most parents are well aware of the notion of praise, but are we going too far? Praise has been promoted as the predominant parental tool to boost children's self-esteem. But like any tool it can be overused so that it becomes ineffective.

Too much praise can be demotivating. If a child is told everything he does is FANTASTIC then how will he ever really know when he has done something that *is* fantastic? Sometimes mediocrity needs to be recognised for what it is – mediocre – rather than boosted to another level.

Encourage more than you praise

Encouragement is a far more powerful esteem-building tool than praise and it doesn't have the adverse side effects. The differences are slim but important. Encouragement focuses on the process of what a child does whereas praise focuses on the end result. Encouraging comments focus on effort, improvement, involvement, enjoyment, contribution or displays of confidence, whereas praise concerns itself with good results. An encouraging parent gives their child feedback about their performance but they ensure the feedback is realistic and they work from positives rather than negatives.

An encouraging parent will note a child's efforts in toilet-training and recognise that mistakes are part of the learning process so they are not too fussed about the results. Praise, however, is saved for a clean nappy and a full potty.

Encouragement recognises that a child is participating and enjoying a game while praise focuses on winning or a fine performance. Okay, the differences are academic and it may seem like splitting hairs, but the results on the potty, in a game or even at the kitchen table should concern children more than they do adults.

As soon as we become more concerned about results than are our children, we move into areas of children's concern and out of areas of our concern. In short, praise is about control and encouragement is about influence.

Encouragement focuses on the following five processes:

1. Improvement: *'You've really come a long way with your spelling.'*
2. Effort: *'You've worked so hard at this. Great to see your effort pay off!'*
3. Contribution: *'Your game today was unselfish.'*
4. Enjoyment: *'It's great to see you enjoy your sport.'*
5. Strategy: *'That was smart to start your project with some planning.'*

Praise with impact

Praise certainly has its place as a parenting tool, but parents need to use it in smart ways, rather than flippantly, insincerely or thrown around like confetti at a wedding, regardless of whether or not it is deserved.

Some children, particularly boys, feel awkward receiving praise unless it is done carefully. It can be misconstrued as manipulative and disingenuous, particularly when it is simply a throw-away line. Time and place is also important; private praise can be more effective than public praise for boys who feel embarrassed being praised in front of their friends or relatives.

There are three types of praise that positively impact children's (as well as adults') behaviour and self-esteem.

1. Descriptive praise

Throw a spotlight on the behaviours that kids do well. Rather than a trite 'well done', draw a word picture of what they did well and let them know its impact. Tell them what you see and how you feel. *'Wow. You have tidied the room really well and put everything back where it should be. It's a pleasure to come into the living room.'* Such a comment genuinely made is more likely to be stored away in a child's memory and drawn on at a later date.

2. Summary praise

Give your child a positive label to live up to by summing up their positive behaviours with one word. 'You really worked hard to finish your project. That's what I call *persistence.*' 'You cleaned up the kitchen without being told. You are a *self-starter.*' 'Persistence' and 'self-starter' become part of your children's self-concepts. Summary praise is great for kids under the age of ten because they still use their parents as reference points. Parental impact of this type is diluted through the teenage years as peer influence has a stronger impact on self-esteem levels.

3. Self-praise

Praise is always a bit more powerful when it comes from within, so allow children to brag a little. *'I did that well.' 'I am really pleased with the way I did that.' 'I did the best I could.' 'I love the art I did at school today.'* Teaching kids to self-praise can be a little tricky but you can start by asking them how they feel about their efforts. When you use descriptive feedback you actually show kids how to self-praise. Self-praise is great to use with kids who always want parental reassurance or approval.

Some kids need to be cued regarding self-praise – *'Are you pleased with yourself because you tried your best in the game?'* Encourage them to say they are pleased with themselves rather than just agree with you. This gets them in the habit of self-praise.

Giving kids feedback

Being an encouraging person doesn't mean that you don't provide kids with feedback about their performance or their behaviour. If neither is up to scratch, then it's incumbent on you to let them know. Also, it's important that you do it in a way that doesn't harm a child's confidence levels and also in a way that helps them improve. These three ideas will help.

1. Focus on the positive first

As much as possible focus on strengths first before giving kids feedback. For instance, *'Max, your spelling is going really well. Let's do some work on your reading.'*

2. Choose your timing

Sometimes well-meaning feedback can be seen as fault-finding when you get the timing wrong. For instance, a parent who corrects a young child's best meal-table setting efforts when he is beaming with pride does more harm than good. Better to wait until next time and give a small reminder then.

3. Make feedback descriptive

Make sure your feedback shows a child how he can do something rather than what he did wrong.

Anchor encouragement to an existing behaviour

Like appreciation, encouragement can easily become part of your family culture. You've just got to get used to giving it every day. If encouragement doesn't come naturally to you, then anchor it to an existing behaviour.

Let me explain. My wife is a wonderful encourager. Encouraging is as easy as breathing to her. She naturally makes people feel good, even brave. Encouragement doesn't come quite so naturally to me, though, so when our kids were young I needed a reminder occasionally. Each time I kissed the kids goodnight I always tried to remember to offer some words of appreciation or encouragement. The kiss goodnight was the anchor or reminder to encourage. By developing that habit, I knew that at least once a day they received some encouragement from me.

Encouragement promotes real confidence in kids – the sort of confidence that enables kids to take learning risks and social risks. As one of my early influences, Austrian psychologist Rudolf Dreikurs, said, 'Like a plant needs water, a child needs encouragement.'

We've got to HAND it to them!

Self-confidence is fed by children's activities and accomplishments. Encouragement and positive thinking achieve little in terms of building a child's self-confidence unless they experience the feeling of success that comes with competence.

Develop a sense of competence

Developing competence is at the heart of boosting kids' confidence. A child's self-esteem comes as a result of their successes and accomplishments. It doesn't come easily; it does not magically appear after hearing a bunch of 'feel good' messages. When children interact successfully with the world they build their bank of accomplishments. When young children learn to wash themselves, even if they can't do it perfectly, that is another experience to add to their repertoire, another experience to support the notion that they are capable, which is the basis of self-esteem. Self-esteem is like an onion: it is built from layers upon layers of accomplishments, with self-worth as its centre.

Competence tends to be self-perpetuating. If a child thinks he is capable based on his experiences of the past, he will in all likelihood succeed. If, however, a child views herself as a failure then she may well act in ways that produce those results and reinforce her own negative view.

The best way to promote competency in kids is to make sure they help out at home. I can't stress enough how important it is that children from the earliest possible age *do things for themselves*. The basic job of parents is to develop independence in their children, and that means making yourself redundant. As a parent that doesn't mean you put your feet up and do nothing. Developing independence in kids takes a great deal of work and patience; it doesn't happen overnight. It does mean that you need to be prepared to teach your child the skills needed – and give them plenty of opportunities to develop the competencies required – for independence.

Self-confidence – a final word

Self-confidence is sometimes confused with bravado, cockiness, even self-assuredness. Self-confidence is closely related to self-belief – that is, the belief that you may be able to achieve or perform but if you don't then failure won't reflect on you. This type of self-confidence takes real courage because you risk failure and exposing all your vulnerabilities for others to see. It's this possibility of failing that holds kids back and prevents them taking learning and social risks. Avoidance of tricky, challenging or new situations where failure is a real possibility becomes a habit that in many ways keeps kids dependent on others to motivate them and persuade them to take risks. Self-confidence is perhaps the trickiest of all traits to develop in kids as they move down the road to independence. The multi-facetted head–heart–hands approach is a parent's best ally when building confidence in children and young people.

chapter six

Emotional intelligence

Get in the mood to achieve

Let's take a minute to ponder where we are.

This is a book that promotes in children real independence, autonomy and self-reliance that they can take into their adult lives. Independence and self-reliance require a certain amount of resilience, because independence-building is always accompanied by some type of risk – whether it be a social risk (fear of rejection), psychological risk (fear of being lost or not finding your way home) or a physical risk (fear of pain, scrapes and bruises that come from falling off a skateboard). Autonomy is achieved when a child becomes responsible or accountable for his behaviour and the choices he makes. The chapter on accountability outlined strategies to use for accountability and responsible behaviour. Confidence and self-belief are central to ongoing success, so for children to truly be independent they need to learn the skills necessary to impact their own confidence levels.

So far we've restricted self-management to what kids can do and how they think. Now it's time to move below the neck and away from their hands to look at the messy area of helping children manage and regulate their emotions. This is the last frontier for parents, and educators, to conquer. As is evident in the previous chapters, as a community we now know a great deal about success-fully managing children's behaviour (without resorting to physical punishment) and we also, thanks to the work of Martin Seligman and Carol Dweck, know about children's explanatory style and the way we think and how our brains work. But there is still a great deal to be learned about how we help children to manage their emotions. In this chapter I will show you how to help children and young people better understand their emotions and have the tools at their fingertips to better manage how they feel.

How do your emotions influence your thinking and behaviour?

If you feel excited reading this, you're probably thinking, *'Come on, get on with it. I just want to get started.'* If you're feeling apprehen-sive, you may be thinking, *'This is so different. I'm not sure I can cope.'* Or you may be thinking, *'I'm not sure this is all it's cracked up to be.'* If you're feeling calm, you might be thinking, *'Hey, this is cool. I'm curious to see what's next. I can't wait to tell my friends . . .'* Feeling and thinking are related. We often operate on a thinking level, ignoring or underestimating the impact of our emotions.

Emotions matter

If you're like me, you live in a very cognitive world, with little cognisance of how your feelings play out. If someone asked me a question such as what I think about the current state of play of parenting, I would probably respond on a cognitive level. *'I think that it's trickier raising kids today because of the massive rate of change, and the personal nature of communication technology makes relationship-building harder . . .'* And away I would go. I don't often answer on an emotional level such as, *'It saddens me that many parents don't experience the same freedom to parent that past generations did.'*

As we discussed in the previous chapter on building self-confidence, it's important to make kids aware of their self-talk and have a number of strategies to help them alter their negative or unhelpful self-talk. You probably know a number of strategies to pass on to your children to help them adjust their thinking. But I'm not convinced that this level of skill and understanding extends to their or our emotional lives. When you hear of an injustice, do you feel the anger rise in you? Do you feel the nuances of your emotions? Do you feel enraged by an injustice or merely irritated by it? These differences are important and will impact your thinking and behaviour. Being aware of the nuances means you have the opportunity to shift your emotional state, rather than be at the mercy of your feelings.

Emotions are information

As a parent your emotions, as well as your child's emotions, give you information that directs your parenting behaviour. Your annoyance about a child's behaviour provides important information about the nature and purpose of the behaviour. Your child's feelings displayed either physically (slumped shoulders due to disappointment or jumping up and down with excitement) or verbally (*'I'm annoyed that my sister won't play with me'*) provide cues about how you should handle a situation. It's easy to take your cues from kids' behaviour or language, and at the same time ignore their emotional response. Emotionally intelligent parenting means we consciously take in the emotional cues that children provide, as well as the cognitive and behavioural cues.

Emotions are neither good nor bad

We tend to think in terms of emotions as good or bad and positive or negative. This is a simplistic view of emotions that suggests that there are some emotions and feelings we shouldn't experience. Being human means that we experience a gamut of emotions across even a single day. How many emotions have you experienced at the day's end? My guess is if you're a parent then you've probably experienced frustration, anger, pride, joy and worry just through your interactions with your children. Not to mention the feelings and emotions evoked by everyone else you've interacted with and other events of the day. It's better to think of emotions in terms of pleasantness and unpleasantness. Some feelings such as joy are obviously pleasant, while sadness is at the other end of the spectrum. Children and young people need to feel comfortable with each feeling even if it's unpleasant. For good emotional health it's critical that we feel comfortable with a range of feelings, and help children to feel comfortable and feel validated regardless of their emotions.

Creating emotionally intelligent families

Professor Marc Brackett, Director of the Yale Center for Emotional Intelligence and the co-creator of RULER, its signature program, says, 'Emotional intelligence needs to become part of the immune system of a family.' I agree. Your family needs to be a place where emotions truly matter. I believe that by paying attention to your own emotional life and the emotional life of your children, then you and your children will be happier, more resilient and more effective in everything they do.

Being a caring, loving parent is great, but it's not enough to equip your kids with the skills they need to thrive when you are not around. Emotional intelligence is at the heart of their personal effectiveness and their positive wellbeing. We need to give our kids the skills to recognise, regulate and express their emotions but first we need to work on our own emotional intelligence as parents.

It starts with recognising the impact of emotions

The recently released movie *Inside Out*, which depicts five emotions in the mind of a young girl, gives life to feelings in a fun, accessible way. It is a wonderful demonstration of why we must put emotional intelligence front and centre in our parenting and teaching. The quickest pathway to happiness and success is the acceptance and recognition of feelings.

This is not a new idea. More than 2000 years ago Socrates reminded his Greek compatriots, 'Educating the mind without educating the heart is no education at all.'

Dr Marc Brackett is more expansive. He says, 'Emotions matter as they drive learning, decision-making, creativity, relationships, and health.'

This is not to say that we ignore children's poor behaviour, neglect to set limits or not ask anything of them in tough times. Accepting and recognising emotions is an added layer in our interactions with kids, which may well be the missing link in building cooperation, connection and resilience.

Parents do hard emotional labour every day

Emotions are messy. They can be loud. They can be hidden. They so often interrupt our well-organised schedules. *'What do you mean you're sad? We're off to watch a movie. It's a happy time!'* Emotions are hard to control and difficult to see.

It's a wonder parents haven't smartened up to emotions earlier because 'good parenting' is hard emotional labour. When your three-year-old throws a tantrum in a supermarket and all you can do is grin and bear it (rather than throw your own tantrum or do what you really feel like, which is to disown your own child) you're doing hard emotional labour.

When you console and contain the hurt of your primary-school child who throws himself at your feet howling that everyone hates him, you are doing emotional labour. Staring down a teenager who looks you straight in the eye while spitting out, 'I hate you!' because you've denied their request to go out is hard emotional labour. Parents do emotional labour all the time. That's one of the reasons it's so draining.

Accepting kids' emotions means we need to listen to them. We need to be mindful of their feelings as well as their behaviours and thoughts, which is what most parents and teachers are conditioned to do. We've built a broad vocabulary around behaviour management featuring terms such as consequences, limits, boundaries and time out, to name a few. And as the perennial 'To smack or not to smack' question shows, we are very willing to debate behaviour management methods, but discussions about emotional management are few and far between.

The limits of many parents' emotional vocabularies are matched by confines in method as well. Most parents, when asked, can provide plenty of ways to raise a well-behaved child, but I suspect many would struggle if asked to name three or more ways to build their children's emotional smarts. This is not a criticism but an acknowledgement of lack of training in the area.

Ask yourself: Who taught you how to recognise, manage and regulate your emotions? If you answered your parents, then lucky you. They've given you the tools you need to have successful relationships, to maximise your earning potential (I kid you not) and to behave like a champ not a chump when playing sport and participating in other competitive or high-performance activities. If you were able to identify any adult who taught you emotional intelligence, I suspect you are in rare company. My guess is you probably couldn't identify anyone, so your emotional intelligence (if you've read this far you have the emotional smarts needed for focus, self-control and concentration) is unconscious, rather than conscious, which makes it hard to teach or pass on to your kids.

So, where do we start? Here are five ideas to help you explore the new frontier of parenting.

1. Listen first
When your child fusses and fumes about some wrong-doing or hurt they've experienced, clear your mind and listen. Avoid trying to fix the situation; just show understanding and compassion. There is no better feeling than being understood.

2. Contain rather than manage (let your kids do the managing)
Children's behaviour can become tangled up in upsets and disappointments. It's hard to separate their behaviour from their

feelings. Sometimes as a loving, caring adult you just have to soak up their feelings, and give them the time and space to soothe their own soul. We don't have to do that for them.

3. Know that emotions can be pleasant and unpleasant

We often place value judgements on emotions by saying some emotions are good or positive (happy, motivated, energised) while some are bad or negative (sad, worried, sullen). Avoid passing judgement in such ways. Recognise that emotions are pleasant or unpleasant and that all emotions are acceptable, whereas some behaviours (such as hurting someone when you are angry) are unacceptable.

4. Build a vocabulary around emotions

Just as feelings have words, so too are there names and terms for an emotionally intelligent parenting method. For instance, I-messages (e.g. *'I feel worried when you don't come home from school on time'*) are a type of communication used by parents and adults who take an emotions-first approach.

5. Help your kids recognise, then regulate, emotions

Ever told a child to calm down only to see their emotions escalate? Kids, like adults, need to recognise their feelings before they can regulate their emotional state, and that's not easy. Emotional recognition is a complex process that takes practice. Even when we are good at it we don't always get it right. Learning to recognise your feelings is a continual process that's best started when young, before the ups and downs of adolescence become a reality.

Emotional intelligence is best learned when it becomes part of your family's culture, or way of doing things; then it will also be passed down from generation to generation. You'll know it's had generational impact when your children identify you as the person who trained them in the skills of emotional intelligence. How cool is that!

Building emotional smarts in children

Emotional intelligence has many components. The best framework I know for helping parents and children understand emotional intelligence is the RULER framework developed by the Yale Center for Emotional Intelligence. The five components of the RULER framework are described below.

1. Recognise emotions

It can be hard for a child or a young person to recognise how they feel. Sometimes unpleasant feelings fester and kids don't realise it and at the end of the day they feel awful or they just explode but you don't know why. The first step in building kids' emotional smarts is helping them recognise the emotions in others. This is usually easy with extreme emotions such as anger as the physical signs are obvious. The face is contorted. The shoulders are high and frequently tense and teeth are often clenched. Behaviourally, anger is expressed through shouting or loud responses and sharp, jerky movements. Sadness is equally easy to spot as facial expressions are generally drawn, shoulders slumped and movements can be glacially slow. Behaviourally, tears and a low, almost whispered, voice is synonymous with making this emotion easy to spot.

Use simple everyday events and situations to highlight emotions. *'Do you think that character is angry? How can you tell?' 'Did you notice how that little girl folded her arms tight and gave her dad a dirty look! I think she was pretty annoyed with him. What do you think?'* By drawing kids' attention to the emotions of others you can help them recognise their own emotions. Children first experience their emotions physically and behaviourally. Kids often describe emotions as 'I get that funny feeling in my tummy', 'I start to feel sick', 'I feel tingly all over!', 'I feel really weird!' It doesn't matter what expression they use; it's important that they recognise the feeling.

Start by helping them recognise the strong emotions – but they don't have to be unpleasant emotions such as nervousness, sadness, anxiety, shock or annoyance. Focus on positive emotions as well, such as happiness, enthusiasm, excitement, cheerfulness and calm. Over time help them identify the internal, physical and behavioural signs of each emotion.

2. Label feelings

Naming an emotion is an important step towards feeling comfortable with it. Even as an adult, when you wake up in the morning perplexed because you feel unsettled, you'll experience a flush of relief when you give that sucker a name – nervous, irritated, discouraged, lonely. Labelling is linked to vocabulary development, so preschool-aged children will in all likelihood possess relatively few feeling words in their emotional vocabulary. 'I'm feeling funny inside' may be the limit to their vocabulary about anxiety. Over time this can be extended to include words such as uneasy, concerned, worried, disturbed, agitated, tense, apprehensive, perturbed, troubled, bothered, overwrought, edgy, worked up, keyed up, stressed, nervous, jumpy, jittery, scared and uptight. The more nuanced the vocabulary the better able we are to shift the way we feel.

3. Understand what caused a feeling

Understanding what causes a feeling has a number of levels. There is the simple *she made me feel this way* approach. For example, a four-year-old is seriously upset because someone has taken their favourite toy or has treated them unfairly. They don't have to look too far for the cause – 'It's my brother!' That may be all that's needed at this age or in this case.

A primary-school child or an adolescent may find it difficult to trace the source of a feeling if there are multiple people or situations involved. Here's an example. Before school one day, nine-year-old Timothy identified that he felt anxious and overwhelmed, which is quite a sophisticated response. He may be alerted to this because behaviourally he was very short-tempered with his mother, and internally he just felt sick and his mind couldn't stop thinking about school. He initially traced his anxiety to the fact that he was sitting a test later that day. But when he thought about this he realised that he wasn't all that concerned about the test. In fact, this child was able to trace his anxiety to a number of causes including ongoing conflict with a few boys at school and his attendance at football practice after school, which he hated with a vengeance. So, in effect, the exam was just the tipping point that may have inflated his already mixed emotions into a very anxious state. This example illustrates that it's not always easy to understand the cause of a deep-seated or overwhelming emotion. The most obvious event or situation may be the trigger for an emotion but there is more to consider. At this point, all that's reasonable is that a child stops and considers what may have led to these feelings. This is a fantastic first step to undertake.

4. Express the feeling in healthy ways

Healthy families work on the premise that there is nothing so bad you can't talk about it but there are some behaviours that are unacceptable. So, when a child comes home from school angry about being teased by his peers it's not acceptable for him to take out his anger on a sibling by hurting, teasing or deliberately ostracising them. Those behaviours are socially unacceptable responses to uncomfortable feelings, yet I see some parents condoning such responses on the pretence that their child simply lost his temper or had been made to feel angry by others – as if lashing out is not the child's fault. This can lead to the lashing out becoming acceptable . . . as long as you are angry or upset. These are not behaviours that children will magically grow out of when they reach adulthood. They're likely to take these ways of responding to high emotion into adulthood and their future family relationships. Frequently, these types of responses escalate rather than decrease, particularly when fuelled by alcohol, drugs and other extenuating circumstances.

So, what are healthy ways to express your feelings? Perhaps the best way to help kids express their worries and anxieties is to allow them to talk about them. This is not always easy because we can sometimes be too rushed and some children become conversational clams when it comes to talking about their worries, fears and anxieties. Here are three big ideas that may help.

Show kids how to talk

The way parents respond to the difficult or unpleasant events in our own lives is on show for children. When we hold things in or lash out verbally we show children how to respond to their feelings. Your ability to talk about how events affect you emotionally as well as how you cope and recover from difficult feelings will provide a blueprint for kids to follow. US researcher Brené Brown in her wonderful work around courage and vulnerability offers great guidance for parents who want their kids to talk about their emotional lives. Brown suggests that parents need to drop their masks of invincibility when they are with their children so that they can connect with children on an emotional level. That doesn't mean that we unload all our worries, frustrations and anxieties on our families. Rather in our conversations or public reflections that we pay as much attention to our emotions as we do to our thoughts and behaviours. For instance, general observations about your day at work over the dinner table may be liberally sprinkled with your feelings as well as your thoughts. *'I was really relieved today that a project that I've been working on for a long time finally came to an end. It probably gave me more headaches and was the cause of more stress and tension than I've felt for a long time.'* Simple acknowledgement about the emotional impact that events have on you can show the way for kids to talk about their emotions.

Focus on emotions first

When children or young people are upset, nervous, angry or overwhelmed by unpleasant feelings, your approach can either shut them down or open up the discussion.

'How do you feel about that?'

This is the first response from a mother when her eight-year-old son told her that his best friend was shifted to another class halfway through the school year. She made emotions her focus in this conversation with her son, inviting him to spill the beans on his thoughts and feelings about an event. Often the conversations we have with kids are pitched at a behavioural level – that is, focusing on children's behaviours and activities and rarely go into the murky world of emotions and feelings. Parents who want to develop emotional intelligence in children and young people will look for opportunities to discuss feelings and emotions. In fact, they'll usually make emotions their first port of call when they talk about difficult stuff.

Make it a habit to talk

It's not a coincidence that the busiest times of the day for Kids Helpline are in the hours immediately after school. Children need to talk about their worries, and in the absence of parents or other trusted adults they will talk to a telephone helpline. It doesn't necessarily have to be after school but we do need to provide children with opportunities to talk and get things off their chests. So, mealtimes, quiet times and even bedtimes can be the ideal opportunities to encourage children and young people to talk on an emotional level.

My mother had a great way of finding out what was on my mind. As an at-home mother she was a woman of her time and was always there when I came home from school. She knew how to make a young boy talk. There was always an after-school snack waiting for me at the kitchen table, and after discarding my schoolbag in my room I'd sit down with her as she had her afternoon cup of tea. She'd always wait until I was comfortable and fed before asking me about my day. Often there was nothing much to report. End of conversation. She wouldn't push the chat. In fact, she wasn't a person for idle chatter, which suited me just fine. Years later she told me that when I had a bad day she couldn't shut me up. She would listen to my tale of woe and she was smart enough not to interrupt the flow with advice or opinions. That occurred later when I was ready.

5. Regulate their moods

Ever had a child in a grumpy mood and she just doesn't know how to make herself feel better? Alternatively, you may have experienced a child who comes home from school so angry that there's steam coming from his ears.

Feeling emotional extremes is part of life, but that doesn't mean we need to stay in those states. Children and young people aren't necessarily hostages to their moods – with a little knowledge and effort they can shift their mood to a more pleasant and productive place.

Help your child to change the way they feel

If your child uses ineffective strategies such as rumination and worry, acting out or self-blame, help them choose more effective strategies from the list below to regulate their emotions. Decide on two or three ideas that seem like a good fit for your child and use them to build their repertoire of emotional intelligence strategies.

1. Take a breath . . . take a few actually

Perhaps the simplest way for a child to feel better, whether it's to settle nerves before a talk or reduce anxiety before meeting new friends, is to take three or four deep breaths. Deep breathing releases dopamine into their system, moving kids toward more pleasant feelings of contentment, happiness and calm.

2. Picture yourself . . .

Encourage your kids to carry a picture of a favourite thing – person, pet or holiday – to help them move to a happier place when needed. Pictures and photos can impact at a deep emotional level. Anyone who carries a picture of a loved one with them will know how powerful a visual reminder can be.

3. Let me entertain you . . .

Watching a movie, reading a book and playing a favourite game are great ways to move moods to more desirable places. These distractions are great for kids' mental health and super mood shifters as well.

4. DO something . . .

Boys are action-oriented and tend to act out their feelings more than girls do. When they are happy they dance and gig around and when they are mad many become aggressive or just more active. Boys also can use action to dissipate emotion or shift their mood to a better place. If they are angry, insist they play an active game or sport to get the energy out. Lethargy, boredom and other passive emotional states too can be shifted through physical activity.

5. Listen to the music . . .

Ever watched a happy scene in a movie and then noticed your whole body tense up when the background music suddenly becomes suspenseful? Music will shift an emotional state quicker than anything else. Encourage kids to change their moods by listening to the music that will help them feel better, or more relaxed, even more inspired. Playing music and singing can have the same effect.

6. They get by with a little help from their friends . . .

Encourage help-seeking behaviours as a way of shifting moods and emotions. It's natural for kids to seek solitude when they feel down or have experienced less than pleasant events. They need time to process events internally. Boys will often visit their caves (aka bedrooms) to process their emotions, while girls are more likely to use a keyboard (formerly it was a diary) to help them work through difficult feelings and events. At some stage they need to emerge and seek the company of others whether for distraction or to share the worries. Seeking the support of family and friends is a fabulous long-term mood changer.

7. Think yourself to a different mood . . .

I remember my mother saying, *'For goodness sake, stop moping about and stop that ridiculous brooding!'* While her take-no-prisoners approach may not be everyone's cup of tea her message has resonance for every parent. If I could think myself into a negative mood, then I could also think my way to a better mood was her notion. She was right. Kids can think happy thoughts by thinking about happier times, happier places and happier events. Their thoughts *do* impact their feelings, so they may as well use them to their advantage.

8. Talk to yourself . . .

Sustained positive self-talk is one of the best ways to move from a place of anxiety to a place of optimism and hope. The trick is for kids to catch their negative self-talk and replace it with a mantra such as, *'I can do this. I've done it before and I'll do it again.'* Change your self-talk, change your moods! The hard part is remembering to do it.

9. Mind the meditation . . .

It's fabulous to see many schools adding mindfulness and meditation to their wellbeing programs. Both are terrific strategies to help kids relax and ease the tensions and stresses of life. Both involve controlling the mental clutter that can overwhelm them, which in turn affects how they feel.

10. Get a good night's sleep . . .

Parents of past generations seemed to be adept at reminding children and young people, *'Get a good night's sleep and things will be right in the morning.'* There's a great deal of scientific evidence to support the fact that your child's emotional health is linked with the amount of sleep they get. With the high number of children currently experiencing anxiety and depression, a great place to start is – a good night's sleep.

Emotional intelligence – a final word

A child's ability to regulate their emotions determines their level of self-management and self-discipline, which are prerequisites for independence. Emotional self-regulation begins in infancy when children self-soothe by sucking their fingers or stroking a blanket to calm themselves down. The expectation for a child to self-regulate increases with age, though many children need considerable adult intervention to assist them to develop emotional acuity. Parents can help children build their emotional smarts by making emotional recognition a feature of normal family life. This includes focusing on emotion rather than behaviour when kids are upset; discussing emotions in everyday conversations; and helping children recognise different feelings and helping them cope or change their emotional states even if just for a short time.

part three

Parenting for independence

In this section I look at two important concepts that will help you bring independence-building to reality. The first is about mindset and the second is about parenting style. Earlier in the book I alluded to the impact that size has on parenting. In a nutshell, the smaller the family the more challenging it is to develop independence and self-reliance in kids. In the next chapter I show you how to approach your parenting using a big-family mindset so that you raise your children with many of the in-built advantages that big families offer in terms of developing independence and resilience.

Then in the following chapters in this section I show you a great way to approach parenting that is easy to remember and, more importantly, easy to apply. I explain how to use non-verbal language to be firm when you need to be – and a great deal of independence-building requires you to be firm. And also I explain an easy way to be the nurturing parent when the situation requires. I'm going to teach you how to bring some cat and dog to your parenting to help you successfully raise your kids to be independent, resilient and socially aware.

111

chapter seven

A big-family mindset

How big was your family? If you were born between the 1970s and 1990s in Australia there's a good chance you had two siblings, because three children was the mean for families in that era. If you were born prior to the 1970s there's a good chance you have three siblings, because four was the mean number for families. And if you go back a generation, there's a good chance that you had two siblings, which was the norm as the Depression followed by World War II both left their mark. Family size is a generational marker.

The number of children in families in Western countries has shrunk dramatically over the past decades. Currently with the average Australian family consisting of 1.8 children, families are smaller than they have ever been. Incredibly, nearly half of Australian families with children under the age of fifteen consist of two children or fewer. The very mention of a family of four kids is enough to gain admiring looks from other parents, mention you have five children and you'll draw gasps of astonishment; and if you have six or more children, people immediately think that you have a step-family.

While there are many factors influencing the size of a family brood, including cultural traditions, religious beliefs and family norms, there are a number of socio-economic factors driving the push toward small families in Australia and other Western countries.

For a start, young adults are not in a hurry to settle down into a steady job and life with their chosen partner. Four decades ago the early twenties was a time to get a job and a partner, hopefully for life, and to have your first child, with twenty-one to twenty-five being the prime child-bearing age group. Now, that has pushed out ten years, with thirty-one to thirty-five being the prime child-bearing age. In 2014 the median age for fathers was thirty-three and the median age for mothers thirty. With couples waiting until their thirties to have their first child, which is a time when the fertility window is already closing, the likelihood of bearing more than two children is less likely. Family size is also now very much an economic decision for people in Western countries, with housing affordability, the high cost of child care and education cited as reasons for limiting the number of children a couple has.

Size matters

Many demographers predict that the trend for one- and two-child families won't change any time soon, so it's clear that small is the norm for most families, with step-families and some cultural groups being the exceptions.

As I have discussed, family size impacts the way children are raised. It's not just the fact that a child in a small family may have only one or no sibling to share his formative years with; parenting style is also affected by the number of children in a brood. In my book *Why First Borns Rule the World and Last Borns Want to Change It* I noted how children in different birth order positions receive different parenting. For instance, I believe that youngest children in a family of three or more should write a letter of thanks to their eldest sibling for breaking their parents in for them because they are generally the recipients of a more relaxed parenting style. Certainly, they are granted more freedom than their first-born sibling, who is generally on the receiving end of a far stricter style of parenting. But size impacts parenting in a number of ways that are perhaps subtle yet no less influential than many people believe.

Size impacts emotional space

The freedom that a child has to act and make decisions without an adult looking over their shoulder and knowing every move they make is affected by family size. This type of emotional space is fascinating to observe. Eldest children have very little of it and youngest children often get it in spades. I remember that when my eldest child came into the world he was the initial repository of all our hopes, dreams and aspirations. Through infancy we followed every little milestone with fascination and noted every breakthrough, from cutting his first teeth to taking his first tentative steps. We thought that we were the only people who had ever had a child, such was our obsession with our son's developmental achievements.

However, I struggle to recall these same moments of magic with my last-born. They happened, but they're not etched in my memory as they are for the eldest. It's not that we weren't thrilled by my youngest's developmental steps. It's more that we were distracted. My youngest had to share the parenting limelight with two older children. Most likely while our youngest was taking her first tentative steps her eldest sibling was learning to ride a two-wheeled bike. Not quite the momentous achievement as taking first steps but big enough to be a diversion for his parents. From birth our eldest has experienced little emotional space from his parents compared to his siblings. We hitched our parenting star to his developmental wagon following every step, every move he made with fascination and interest. Our first-born is not alone; we are typical of many parents. The photo album of an eldest child is full of happy childhood moments and full of firsts. But mainly they are full of moments captured of them alone or alone with you. Compare this to the photo album of a youngest child and they are lucky to have a photo of them alone or with you. There will invariably be other siblings or family members in the frame.

Eldest children are generally highly visible. They are the ground-breakers for their parents, and they experience greater pressure to meet parent expectations than any other member of the family. As the family standard bearers they get very little emotional space from their parents. Youngest children by comparison are less visible. They experience more relaxed parenting and don't have nearly as much pressure to live up to family standards. In short, they get plenty of emotional space from their parents. The larger the family, the more space that youngest children receive from their parents.

In families of four or more children, parent attention and aspiration is shared around. It's never shared evenly, because first-borns carry a greater burden of parent expectation than other birth-order positions. Also, parents will give their youngest child more freedom to make their own choices than they gave their first. But in the larger family the parent focus on individual children is less intense than in families of two or fewer children, where parents are more likely to focus like a laser beam on the activities and performance of each child.

The amount of emotional space children receive in big families is significant, offering a massive advantage in terms of independence-building for those who receive more of it. It means that children have the freedom to negotiate their environment, resolve their own problems and make simple decisions that impact their physical and immediate needs without constant parent intervention and control. By default they become less dependent on their parents than do children in small families. Parent dependency can in some places be replaced by dependency on siblings, but this is usually not as strong or potentially smothering as a relationship with a parent.

The nature of the relationship in small families is usually very intense, with parents being involved in the minutiae of children's lives. A parent of a small family will invariably know whether their children had breakfast on any given morning and more than likely know what they ate. A parent in a family of four may know if each child had breakfast but they may not know what they ate. A parent of a family of six or more probably wouldn't know if everyone ate breakfast and certainly wouldn't know what every child ate. That type of space creates opportunities for children to take greater responsibility for themselves, and also for each other. I'm not advocating that parents in big families abrogate responsibility or neglect their children, but the very nature of large families means that they can't physically attend to all children all the time. This space is often filled by other siblings, who will invariably look after the wellbeing of each other when given the chance.

Alternatively, children become resourceful and start to find their own ways to look after themselves. In the example of the breakfast, when given space it may be that a parent discovers that some children eat breakfast on the run, some may miss breakfast altogether and some may make unhealthy choices. This requires parents to make gentle adjustments, working with children individually to reset their breakfast routines. I suspect in big families many parents would advise children about their expectations and do their best to supervise – maybe even delegate supervision to an elder sibling – but they wouldn't be overly worried or concerned about children making the right choices every time as they would in a small family. In families of two or fewer it's difficult not to want to be the perfect parent. In big families parents are more likely to operate according to the 'It's Near Enough' policy and recognise that children will survive even though they may miss the odd breakfast (or lunch) here or there.

Pester power lives in small families

In small families pester power lives because it's easy for one persistent, strong, even manipulative voice to be heard. 'Mum, I want . . .' can wear you down when it's said repeatedly despite the fact that you've denied a request. In small families, particularly in single-parent small families, this persistent pestering is commonplace. The bigger the herd the harder it is for individual voices to be heard above the din. Besides, large families are more hierarchical by nature, which has a dampening effect on pester power.

Size affects relationships

During the past few years a flourishing parenting-advice industry has emerged. Bookshelves now buckle under the weight of so many parenting tomes in bookshops and libraries. The blogosphere is thick with parenting bloggers dispensing advice about all sorts of family and child-related topics. And current-affairs and breakfast-television programs, as well as their radio counterparts, have their parenting experts. Parents can feel completely overwhelmed, particularly when confronted with contradictory advice. But most parenting advice is directed squarely at promoting the parent–child relationship, and often neglects the importance of the sibling relationship.

The parent–child relationship is not the only family relationship that impacts kids. The sibling relationship is the forgotten relationship. It will last longer than the parent–child relationship and is just as influential on children's development as the parent–child relationship. Over the past decades we've de-emphasised the sibling relationship relative to the parent–child bond, which is to the detriment of families and to kids themselves.

In families of four or more siblings the relationships are many, varied and complex. Each child has a relationship with each other as well as with each parent. In a family of four children and two parents, there are fifteen individual relationships. That's a lot of relationships to negotiate and a great deal of potential conflict as well. More importantly, that's many more social learning experiences for a child than he would experience in a small family.

We learn so much through our sibling relationships; perhaps as much if not more than through our parents. In large families children learn how to resolve conflicts and how to conduct friendships. They also learn how to defend themselves and how to forgive. Sisters teach boys about girls, and brothers teach sisters about boys. Older siblings learn how to nurture younger siblings, which gives them an early experience of parenting. Younger siblings learn a great deal about the wider world, often before they are ready, from their elder brothers and sisters. A household with multiple siblings is a household full of personalities that are forever in motion.

In small families the parent–child relationship rules. It's a more competitive environment when there are two siblings, because 100 per cent of your rivals sits across the breakfast table every morning. Parents are better able to develop healthy one-on-one relationships with their children when they lead small families, which is a distinct advantage. As a general rule, the larger the family, the less likelihood there is for parents to develop strong bonds with every child. However, sibling relationships frequently form a substitute to parent–child relationships in large families.

Size affects family management

The parenting in small families tends to be a very individual endeavour, while parenting in large families focuses more on the gang. Parents in small families operate under the principle of *'What's best for the child?'* In large families parents operate under the principle of *'What's in the best interests of the family?'* It's fascinating to observe how the discipline process differs between small and large families. In a family of one or two children parents will invariably go to great pains to discipline a wrong-doer, discovering and punishing the culprit who instigated the dispute. In large families children are more likely to work out their disputes themselves, and if parents did intervene the whole family would more than likely experience the consequences for one child's wrong-doing. This strategy often brings siblings closer together as they close ranks against the parent who had the audacity to punish the whole gang.

Being brought up in a large family means that children continually hone their conflict-resolution skills on their siblings, which is great preparation for negotiating the many social situations that children encounter at childcare, preschool, school and beyond. Most large families are hierarchical groups with their own pecking order defined by a mixture of birth order, personality, temperament, gender and circumstance. It's not just the top-down nature of families where the oldest (who is often the most experienced, biggest, most powerful sibling) rules the sibling roost, but often parents favour one child over another, giving her more attention and positive energy than other siblings. This has always been the way of families, but we don't feel overly comfortable with this concept in our modern democracies, where everyone is supposedly created equal and has equal opportunity. 'Know thy place' is the ethos in most large families, with a great deal of sibling energy and hostility going into making sure everyone remains in their allotted place in the family hierarchy.

Small families have their advantages

So far I've made a great case for big families being the only family type that can raise independent kids. Obviously this is not true. My argument has been that large families, those with four kids or more, are by their very nature well placed to develop real independence, autonomy and resilience in children.

There are, however, plenty of advantages for a child being brought up in a small family. Relatively easy access to a caring parent is a huge positive that is not always afforded a child being raised in a large brood. It's only a negative when parents don't give children opportunities to sort out a problem themselves and instead take the problem away. In large families some children can easily get lost, whereas parents in small families are often more aware of when there are significant problems that need parent attention, or professional assistance. From time to time, such as when changing from primary to secondary school, children benefit from close individual attention, which a small family is better positioned to provide. So, small families have lots of benefit too. But if independence is your goal, my advice is to adopt a big-family mindset when raising your children.

Preschools and schools are like big families

A big-family mindset has limitations. How do you make an only child wait her turn in a conversation at the meal table? How do you encourage a girl in a small family to share her toys and possessions when her only sibling is a brother who doesn't care much for her toys anyway? How do you provide an opportunity for the youngest child in a small family to look after a sibling?

Fortunately, early-learning centres and schools offer many of the learning and socialisation opportunities that small families can't provide. They, in effect, operate like large families. Generally, children don't have the same access to adults as they do at home, which forces them to find their own way to resolve many of their social problems. A territorial dispute – such as when one child enters the play zone of another and won't leave when asked – is more likely to be sorted out by children in a school or early-learning setting because access to teachers or carers is more difficult. I suspect that most children know intuitively that solving children's territorial disputes is relatively low on the list of priorities for teachers or carers. Whether by design or by accident the benign neglect that children can experience in educational settings can provide them with the space and opportunities to draw on their own resources. As Jeffrey Kluger, author of *The Sibling Effect*, noted, when children are left to their own devices to resolve relationship issues they generally do so more efficiently and more fairly than when adults step in and solve problems on their behalf.

To advocate or not on behalf of your child

I think as parents you need to resist the natural temptation to advocate on behalf of your child when you learn that they are experiencing social problems and difficulties in a setting outside of the family. Children need the opportunity to resolve their social problems themselves in their own time. Help them process what may have happened in a situation or incident and give them some tips and tricks to handle a similar situation should it arise again, but resist the temptation to fight your child's fight for them. Children of all ages generally develop their own ways of managing disputes and sorting out their conflict with others. That, of course, doesn't make it easy when your four-year-old comes to you with a tale of woe about another child always pushing in front of him when playing; or a seven-year-old who discovers his play lunch goes missing; or a twelve-year-old who experiences rejection from her previously best friend. The first emotional response in many ways is to go to the preschool or school and make everything better. The feeling may be natural, but we don't always act on feelings.

Better to take an empathetic approach when kids experience difficulties. '*I get it*' is the most helpful response you can give a child of any age who is upset by the actions of others. Then ask good questions to find out if a dispute or conflict is a one-off event or an ongoing issue. Ascertain your child's part in the situation and, importantly, do your best to understand if your child has the power or the wherewithal to resolve the problem. If you think that there is nothing they can do to resolve a continuing dispute, then it may be time to advocate on your child's behalf by initiating a meeting with a teacher, carer or coach.

Six ways to a big-family mindset

Raising your small family with a big-family mindset is a fine mantra, but how to make it happen is a different story. I've outlined six principles to help you apply a big-family mindset to your parenting.

Love your children confidently

There are two ways you can love your child – you can love them helplessly or you can love them confidently. No one sets out to love their child helplessly. Every parent I know wants to raise kids to be confident, fearless and brave yet sometimes practice doesn't match our goals. We want our kids to be responsible yet when they don't complete their homework on time we make excuses for them or initiate a discussion with teachers about the validity of homework. We want our kids to be independent yet we pack their school bags for them each day when they are capable of doing so themselves. It's in the myriad of such small ways that adults develop a sense of learned helplessness in their children.

The alternative is to love our kids confidently. That is, we treat children as we want them to be. We give them real responsibility for their everyday lives and refuse to rescue them when life gets hard, when it gets tedious and even when they say things to make us feel guilty. That's a big challenge, I know, but loving kids confidently comes naturally when redundancy is your goal as a parent.

Stepping away

Some years ago when I picked up one of my children from pre-school, a well-meaning assistant said she had something serious to discuss with me. This child had some form, particularly for being too aggressive in dealing with conflict situations with other children. I swallowed hard, thinking, *What now?* The assistant said I should know that my child wasn't sharing nicely like the other children. This revelation wasn't accompanied by any behavioural advice whatsoever. *Is that all?* was my first thought; this was small beer indeed for this child. I thanked the assistant, however I left thinking I wanted to know about serious indiscretions not every single thing that my child had done. It just wasn't necessary – kids need the space that comes from their parents not knowing their every indiscretion.

In the current climate of accountability and performance that exists in childcare centres and schools, there is a great deal of recording and measuring of a child's behaviour and development. Little is left to chance. I applaud the attention to detail but it's concerning that normal developmental delays are overplayed and children whose behaviour doesn't fit the norm can become the focus of unwarranted worry and attention from parents.

My suggestion is to use the big-family filter when problems are brought to your attention. When you notice that your child has a problem, or someone draws your attention to a child's behavioural or learning issue, ask yourself: *Would I find this out if my child was a member of a big family?* If the answer is affirmative, I suggest that the problem is significant because it has passed through many significant filters just to reach you. If your answer is negative, then maybe, just maybe, the issue is minor and deserves the chance to be fixed without your input. Sometimes a problem needs time to work itself out; or a child needs the space to work out a problem themselves.

Similarly, there is a tremendous pressure now for well-meaning parents to attend children's sporting, leisure and performance pursuits. After all, that's what good parents do, isn't it? This is all well and good when children are very young. They love to have their parents watch them play or participate in their activities. As children move through primary school and into secondary, pull back from going to every activity. Let them know that you are interested in their activities but you are not attached to what they do. Show interest but give them space to perform well or poorly without you being there. Also encourage children to make their own way to after-school activities – this means they may have to walk, use public transport or negotiate a ride with other parents, which is all great practice for kids. This is the type of experience that children in large families have because their parents can't make it to every child's weekend or after-school activity.

Letting go

Perhaps the hardest part of being a loving parent is relinquishing responsibility for your child's wellbeing and happiness. But parenting is one long process of letting go. Sometimes the hand over is small; sometimes it's significant, like the time I let go of taking responsibility for my son's success at school. For much of this child's secondary-school years my wife and I were locked in a battle with him over his schooling. It seemed that we were more worried about his school success than he was. During every mid-year parent–teacher interview we were given a similar 'he needs to knuckle down and work' spiel from frustrated teachers. We'd then relay the message to him at home following the interview. He usually would knuckle down and work so that his marks generally improved toward the end of the year. But it was hard work for all concerned.

In his second-last year of school we attended the mid-year parent–teacher interviews and received the usual 'must work harder' message. By this stage my wife and I were thoroughly sick of hearing this, but also tired of the continuous job of motivating our son to work. We both looked at each and said, 'No more!' For the first time we had a serious talk with him about leaving school and looking for an apprenticeship. He was sixteen and therefore legally able to leave, and this was no parent bluff. It came as quite a shock to this young man. It seemed that he wasn't quite ready to leave school, so for the first time in many years he began to take his schooling seriously. There was no need for the usual motivational talk. He really applied himself over the long term. What was the magic formula? We didn't know it at the time, but by letting go we handed the responsibility for his future over to him.

The best way to develop responsibility in children is to give them responsibility. Our job as parents is to make it easy for our children to take responsibility rather than take the responsibility away. The distinction is subtle but powerful. Your true attitude is usually broadcast through your non-verbal communication. You may say to a child, *'It's your job to pack your lunch and I don't care too much if you leave it at home.'* But your tone of voice and facial expression will give away your real intentions. If it's said with an air of nonchalance, you are more likely to convey

127

that the responsibility really is being given to your child. If you employ a needy tone of voice and a doubtful facial expression, your child will pick up that Mum or Dad doesn't really mean what they say.

Letting go of responsibility happens more naturally for parents in large families than in small families. Children in large families are more likely to get themselves and each other up, prepare their own school lunches and generally take responsibility for more aspects of their everyday lives than children in smaller families. Size quite simply affords greater space and opportunity for children to accept greater accountability for their lives. Parents in small families need to be more conscious of letting go and giving greater responsibility to kids.

Letting go means that children will mess up and make mistakes. Inevitably they will sleep in when they are responsible for getting themselves out of bed each morning, and school buses will be missed; lunches will be left at home and homework will be forgotten. Taking responsibility means that children should not be continuously rescued by well-meaning parents who drive them to school when they sleep in, who take forgotten lunches to school or who write notes excusing kids from doing their homework when they forget. Parents need to let go of the need to rescue children from potentially difficult situations of their own making. It's not easy but it needs to happen if we want kids to be resilient and develop their own resources.

Separating yourself from your child

One of the big differences between being a parent and being teacher, friend or interested adult in a child's life is that parents generally have significant hopes and dreams for their children.

These aspirations may be unspoken but they exist. Many parents tell me that all they want is for their child 'to be happy' – but I don't buy this for a minute. Parents may want their kids to be happy but they also want a whole lot more. They generally want them to be successful in the areas of life that they value or have experienced success in, or even lack success in. For instance, there's an unconscious expectation from many tertiary-educated parents that their children will also be tertiary educated; anything less and children may be seen as failures, unless of course they experience success in another field. It's my observation that those children who don't follow the family way need to experience significant success in areas not valued by parents to satisfy their aspirations. Stars of the stage and sports field usually exceed their parents' expectations regardless of their original aspirations. The trouble with parent aspirations is that they can stifle children when they don't match their children's interests and abilities.

As I mentioned earlier, parent aspiration is shared around in large families, but heavily focused on just one or two children in small families. This presents a problem when parents mix their aspirations with those of their children. It can lead to excessive pressure for children to succeed in areas where they have no interest or aptitude. Parents, in effect, can hoist their aspirations on to their children and find it difficult to separate themselves from their children's success. When a child does well on the sporting field it not only reflects well on them, but there is also a type of glory for parents. Similarly, a child's top marks in school reflect well on parents, giving them a chance to perhaps vicariously experience the success that they didn't achieve as kids. In a way all parents live vicariously through their children, but it's important not to step over the line whereby it becomes almost impossible to separate yourself from your child.

The space from children afforded to parents in large families means that it's easier for them to be objective about their children, and not pin their parenting success on their children's achievements. A large family will invariably produce a diverse tribe with different interests, aspirations and personalities. There is a good chance that a family of six children will produce at least one child who follows in a similar type of occupation to their parents, or one that they value highly. There will be one child who follows a completely different occupation. For instance, if parents are professionals such as a doctor or lawyer, it is likely that at least one child will follow in their footsteps but also that at least one child will be a tradesperson or in the performing arts. Knowledge of birth order suggests that it will be the youngest child who is most likely to forge their own path, because parent aspirations are not as strong for youngest children.

It is difficult for parents in small families to separate their ambitions from those of their child, but effective parenting demands it. It's imperative to step back from your child and be objective when a teacher gives you a less than positive assessment of your child's behaviour. It's imperative to not care more about winning or good performance than your child does when he hits the sporting field. And it's imperative that you can separate yourself from a young person who announces that they are gay so that you can accept them despite the fact that this aspect of their sexuality was possibly never on your parenting radar. A healthy relationship always has a well-defined separation so that both people can choose their own path. The same principle applies to the parent–child relationship. The following chapter shows you how.

Don't put all your eggs in the parenting basket

Remember the days before children or a partner entered your life? You had a life full of interests, hobbies and social possibilities. No matter where you were on the career path, what type of job you had or whether you worked for yourself or were looking for work, your life revolved around YOU! If you're a fitness freak, you had plenty of time to visit the gym, play your chosen sport or pursue your particular passion. If you're a social butterfly, you were free to party on, party hard or just opt for a quiet night in if that was your preference. If you are more the quiet type who prefers the company of a few rather than many, enjoys curling up with a good book or vegging in front of your favourite screen, you were probably free to do so.

Then a partner came along and suddenly you broadened your focus from YOU to US. You had to make room for someone else in your life. This probably meant some adjustment, but I suspect like most people YOU still found a place for your interests and passions, while putting time and energy into US – you and your partner.

In the days before children you were a person first, a partner second. When you had children all this was thrown upside down. You became a parent first, partner second and a person last. This happens to most mothers and many fathers at the birth of their first child. Your baby becomes the total focus of your life as much of your waking life is taken up with feeding, nursing and resting and recovering so you can continue feeding, nursing and tending to your baby's needs. At some point you and your partner look knowingly at each other and you know it's time to pay attention to your partnership. (Note some parents never reconnect, placing their partnership at risk.) At this point you begin to make space

131

for each other, but you can never go back to the way you were. If you are a loving couple you naturally want to share the joys and frustrations of parenting. Your conversations, if they don't centre around your new baby, become laced with snippets about the baby's development. Suddenly you relate to each other as parents rather than as people with personal interests and a life outside of family and work. Many parents never return to life before children when they were a person first and partner second. When you look at child-rearing through the redundancy lens, putting yourself front and centre becomes an imperative that you need to pursue.

Let's explore how.

Imagine that you have a family of three – yourself, a partner and a child. You have sufficient food but it's low in quality. Your sole source of protein is a dozen eggs delivered each week, and distributing the eggs is your responsibility. How will you divide the eggs each week? Will you provide them equally? Will you give more to yourself, to your partner or to your child? If you are like many parents I meet you'll give yourself the least amount, your child the most, and the number your partner receives will fall somewhere in between.

Now imagine each egg represents a unit of your time and energy. Most parents I meet will give their children most of their time and energy; they save some for their partner and then give whatever is left over to themselves. Of course, there are competing demands on our time and energy such as paid work, broader family commitments and unexpected events that are thrown our way. The point is most parents these days exist in a state of exhaustion from the time their first child enters the world until the time they set up their own home – which in today's terms is around the age of thirty. Days are spent looking after children's various needs so that the person you used to be becomes buried beneath the weight of daily commitments. Go to the gym? You're kidding! Have a night out with my friends? I wish! Spend a day curled up with a good book? Yeah, right!

In my book *Thriving!* I wrote about the importance of taking time for yourself and also making time for your partner and other relationships in your life. I stated, '. . . if you do attend to all areas of your life, you are likely to become a more effective parent. You'll be more interesting to be with and have more energy to bring to your child-rearing.' The conversations I've had with parents in the seven years since I wrote this follow a similar pattern – 'It sounds good but making it happen is difficult.' I agree! In the current climate that places incredibly high expectations on parents, taking time for yourself is vital. How can a parent take a few extra hours each week when in all likelihood they are working full- or part-time; spending most of their free time taking children from one after-school activity to another; not to mention the expectation of spending quality time with the whole family and also with each individual child. There are only so many hours in a day! Something has got to give – and usually it's parents.

Before even considering carving out some time for you, it's necessary to address the elephant in the room. That, of course, would be parental guilt. That tricky little emotion that's always there, whispering in your ear to be the best possible parent for your child. Guilt can be a useful emotion if, for example, it motivates parents to spend some of their time in their children's company rather than all their time at work. That's guilt working its good thing!

However, guilt can be detrimental if it drives us to spend all our waking hours in the service of children. It's detrimental when it drives us to buy our children everything they want in an effort to assuage guilt. It's detrimental if you don't expect your kids to help at home because you feel guilty about it. Guilt is the enemy of redundancy. It causes us to make emotive, short-term decisions that aren't necessarily in the long-term best interests of kids. Guilt stops us from letting go of many of our parental responsibilities and passing them over to our kids. Guilt also stops us from taking some time for ourselves, because that usually means taking time away from being in the service of kids.

So, you need to stare down guilt before you even attempt to create some time for yourself and your partner. Don't let it win. Know you are important and that your child will survive without you. You are doing your child a favour if you expect them to wait rather than give them what they want, when they want it. Better still, do away altogether with the notion of being a good parent and replace it with the concept of being a responsible parent – that is, someone who is hell-bent on raising a responsible child.

Time for you

It's difficult to come up with hard and fast rules around personal time, but the work of Alfred Adler, the father of individual psychology, is a useful starting point. He maintained that those people who lived the happiest, most fulfilled lives actively attended to three external factors of life – family, work and social or community obligations. When we neglect one area at the expense of others for an extended period, our general wellbeing suffers. There is a fourth area that needs our attention and energy as well – our personal wellbeing. Neglect your physical, intellectual and spiritual wellbeing and you won't function effectively in the three external areas. Here are three ways to create some time for YOU.

Free time each day (when you're not exhausted): Free, unorganised time without external constraints is an essential building block for good mental health. Kids need it. Depending on their age and inclination they will play, muck around, spend time on a screen, listen to music, build a fort or cubby. Most children have little trouble filling their free time. Many adults, however, can feel decidedly uncomfortable when we have some free time on our hands. Surely, we must do something productive! With a to-do list the length of our arm how can we possibly take half an hour off to mess around, chill or do nothing at all? Well, good mental health demands it. Besides, if you want to put your parenting hat on by taking some daily R&R you are modelling good mental health for kids rather than modelling exhaustion as a status symbol.

Do something that energises you: Energy out, energy in! Here's a tricky question. What do you have in your life that you are so passionate about that when you do it you lose all sense of time? Whether it's restoring an old car, organising the school or community art fair or joining a book club, everyone functions better when they have their own interests outside their family and working life. If you've lost that part of your life, take some time to discover a passion or interest.

Do something creative and playful: Brené Brown in her ground-breaking work on vulnerability found that without exception those people who live happy, fulfilled lives do something creative in their free time. She maintains that there is a creative side in all of us that is often pushed aside in our modern task-oriented, work-to-put-bread-on-the-table lives. *'If it's not productive, I'm not doing it'* is the mantra that too many people live by. Denying this creative, even playful side is a recipe for well-being disaster. In fact, Brown goes as far as saying the opposite of play is not work, but depression. That is, if you strip creativity and playfulness completely from your life, which so often happens with parents today, then you are at risk of experiencing anxiety and even depression, particularly as you reach your forties, which is a stage when those who have lived by the all-work-and-no-play credo start to experience the negative impact of such a lifestyle. So, if you identify with anything I've written in this paragraph, it may be time to join a local choir, sign up for an art class or take salsa lessons with your partner. Anything to put some creativity, play and – dare I say it – joy into your life.

Time for your partner

You may not be able to recapture those times with your partner when you spent hours in each other's company, talking about seemingly insignificant matters that opened windows into each other's personalities. But you can recapture some intimacy, by building regular partner time into your life. Strong partnerships recognise and celebrate their past history, share their present lives together and shape their future by working toward shared goals. They have interactions that attend to the past, present and future.

Here are some interactions to consider.

Daily catch-up: Try to spend some time together each day without kids where you catch up on each other's day. When the kids are in bed it's tempting for couples to retreat to their cocoon of a book, television or computer and they never actually catch up and talk about their day. Couples easily fall out of the habit of sharing some of the minutiae of their daily lives and wonder why they've grown apart. Lack of daily communication leads to lack of intimacy and can cause both genders to seek solace with someone else.

Weekly or fortnightly rendezvous: Arrange to meet with your partner on a regular basis to share a coffee, a drink, or even a meal. Ideally this should occur outside the house. Change the venue and activity but try to keep the time constant. The key is to ritualise your rendezvous. It should be a regular entry in the diary of both partners.

Night or weekend away: Book the kids into their grandparents or friends for babysitting and make sure you have a night or two with your partner at least twice a year. You don't have to stay in an expensive place, although it is an option. If your budget is stretched, stay at home and prepare a special meal. Make the weekend something special for you and your partner. My wife and I have made an art form of nights and weekends away. We began spending a weekend away once a year before our children started school. We'd swap the organising and keep the expectations reasonable in terms of where we went. It was the fact that we got away rather than the location or surroundings that we both valued. This grew to two weekends a year and gradually extended to include more extensive travel together as the children became more independent.

What about sole parents?

Those who parent solo need to get away too. Children can easily become the focus for single parents. This is often more evident in the early days after a separation, when children fill a void left by a partner's departure. Social invitations and offers for assistance can easily be refused and participation in social events can decrease.

Sole parents who are the custodial parent generally get little respite, particularly if the kids are school-aged. It's important for personal wellbeing to have a break from the children at least once a week. Not only will kids benefit from having a refreshed parent they may also appreciate being in the company of someone different. But it's hard sometimes to get away. A good support network is important.

Put big-family values into your family frame

So, what common traits and characteristics do your children share? It can be difficult to determine when children are in early childhood because the differences between children are often more apparent than the similarities. As children move into primary school and beyond through the secondary-school years the similarities are easier to spot, and they are important because they indicate the values and characteristics you value as a parent. Family constellation (birth-order position) will account for many of the differences between children. For instance, if your eldest child is responsible, well behaved and cooperative, there is a reasonable chance that your second child will be quite the opposite – a carefree, competitive character. Like niche marketers, children will play to their strengths within a family to attract attention from parents.

On the surface, this may make well-intentioned parenting seem pointless because you may focus on a particular value or characteristic but it won't necessarily be adopted by each child. This is only partly valid. Children invariably adopt the dominant values they are exposed to within their family in childhood. Each child in a family may display those values to different degrees, but they are drivers of their behaviour and attitudes. So, if each child in a family has a high work ethic, even if to varying degrees, then high work ethic is most likely part of your family frame. Take a moment to reflect on the commonalities between your children, or, if applicable, the values and attitudes you share with your own siblings. These will be indicative of the impact of the parenting that they, or you, received. The predominant values that kids learn in their family usually stay for life. Those values will be stronger in some children than others, but all children will relate to them.

Big-family values

From my research into what makes healthy families tick I've noticed that the following five values constantly occur.

1. Independence

Your kids won't magically become independent unless you place independence firmly in your family frame. If each child works hard at whatever they do, they've probably picked up a high work ethic from their parents. Hard work is more than likely modelled by one or more parents and your family's proprietary language is littered with phrases such as, *'Hard work never hurt anyone,' 'The harder you work the more successful you'll be,'* and *'Work your way through obstacles.'* Similarly, when all children in a family are self-sufficient, it's indicative of a parenting style that promotes independence and autonomy. Independence becomes a core strategy so that self-sufficiency is modelled and the family's language is peppered with words and phrases that promote self-sufficiency and autonomy – phrases such as, *'It's your choice,' 'That's something you can do yourself'* and *'No excuses. You need to take responsibility for your own behaviour.'*

2. Resilience

Resilience refers to children's ability to cope and bounce back from hardships, frustration and difficulties they face on a regular basis. Most resilience experts agree that children have a natural instinct toward resilience but this can be adversely affected by experiences in early to middle childhood. These include a traumatic event, mental illness, lack of parental support and an overprotective or smothering parenting style. The easiest way to promote resilience is to offer your child unconditional love and support; do all in your power to provide a safe, predictable family environment; look for opportunity to build your child's coping capacities and strengths; and build your family's proprietary language around resilience. This includes phrases such as: 'Hang in there!' 'This too shall pass!' 'Don't let this disappointment spoil everything.'

3. Shared responsibility

Generally, families that function well are guided democracies or benign dictatorships. They work best when parents take on the executive function, running the family like a joint enterprise, with all members regardless of age having a stake in the operation. That means that kids according to age and interest have some say in how their family operates, how the family cares for its members and how individuals behave and contribute to their group.

It's not up to parents to resolve every problem, rather it's up to parents to facilitate the group to resolve issues and for kids to assist and care for each other. If a child has a behavioural or learning issue, the whole group can have some sort of stake in assisting that child. Families work well when everyone contributes and helps out if individuals have problems or difficulties.

4. Contribution

Kids will belong in their families in two ways – through contribution and active participation or as passive receivers of care and attention. Children with additional needs may not have the capacity to contribute as much as others, but their participation can still be positive and valued. The key is to give kids an opportunity to contribute to their own wellbeing, as well as that of their siblings and the family, through chores and other domestic responsibility, without being paid. Children in large families by default usually have to help around the house, look after siblings and take responsibility for their possessions without an expectation of being paid.

5. Social interest

Social interest is a wonderful concept that ideally every family adopts as a value. It means acting for the good of the group – whatever group you are in. All children have a need to develop social interest because they are egocentric. The world revolves around them – quite rightfully too. With maturity they develop greater empathy for others – as well as a realisation that the world *doesn't* revolve around them – and they begin to take into consideration the greater social good when they behave. The family is a great learning ground for the development of a child's social interest. They must learn that they need to fit in to what happens around them. The sense of belonging and wellbeing that kids get from heightened social interest is profound.

These values frequently occur quite naturally in big families. In fact, the greater space and freedom given to children by parents in large families encourages self-reliance and natural resilience. Large families almost invariably function around the predominant values of shared responsibility, contribution and social interest. In the absence of these values large families become quite dysfunctional. This notion gives raising a small family with a big-family mindset real legs.

Become more comfortable with risk

Earlier in this section I briefly addressed the elephant in the room when it comes to stepping back and allowing children to become independent – that is, parental guilt. Parental guilt can inadvertently lead to children's greater dependence on adults. Your attitude to children experiencing risk can equally determine their levels of independence. The trouble with leading a small family is that you can know too much for your own comfort.

There's no getting away from it: if you are going to raise your child to become self-reliant and refrain from spoonfeeding them, you need to have a healthy, realistic attitude toward risk. I'm not referring to five-year-old-boy-climbs-up-ladder-and-jumps-off-the-roof type of risk. That's simply reckless. But a great deal of growing up and growing confidently away from parents involves a certain amount of physical and social risk. I'll be blunt. As a community we're far too protective of our children and young people. Most parents admit that their own parents gave them more freedom to navigate their neighbourhoods than they give their children at the same age. They regret the highly organised, sanitised lives that their children lead compared to their own, yet few will grant their children the same degree of freedom they experienced. Anecdotally, it would seem that fear for children's safety is an overriding reason for placing many restrictions on them both inside and outside the home.

Risk is good for kids

Children are first and foremost heuristic learners. That is, they learn to modify their behaviour through experience. The trouble is that many of the experiences can be unpleasant, uncivil and at times downright hurtful. Tell some children not to pat a dog, and they'll ignore your good advice, preferring to find out for themselves why they should keep their hands away. *Yes, he bites. I'll remember that for next time.* Once bitten twice shy is the maxim for some kids; other children, though mindful of past lessons, will still put their hand out – they'll just be smarter and offer food this time around. Allowing children to experience risks that are inherent in an environment will develop a greater understanding of risks and enable them to modify their behaviour accordingly.

The lessons some children learn in the school of hard knocks can be bitter, which makes it tough for parents. However, it's our role to point out risk, and of course to protect kids outright if the risks are too great. From a redundancy-parenting perspective we also should do all in our power to skill kids up to negotiate risk safely and support them when they run up against hardships. Experiencing risk helps kids overcome their fears.

Many fears – such as fear of separation, fear of the dark and fear of new situations – are normal and developmental. Other fears – such as fear of the dentist, fear of new social situations and fear of dogs – are more individual. They are often learned, or heightened due to experience.

Fear is okay

Navigating fear is part of growing up. Fear plays an important role in keeping us safe: it makes us cautious and causes us to prepare for new or risky situations. That preparation may be physical (*'I'll walk on the other side of the street to avoid that mean dog'*) or psychological (*'I'll be brave when I visit the dentist'*).

Sometimes normal, healthy fears are confused with anxiety. Fear is unhealthy if it overwhelms kids, dominating their thinking and behaviour, or if it paralyses and prevents them from participating in everyday life. Fear is normal if it makes children wary, but not if it overwhelms.

Fears need to be faced

It's important to remember that fear decreases (and sometimes disappears) with positive experiences. Walk past a scary dog a few times without being bitten and a child eventually learns that it's not so scary after all. Give enough speeches in front of groups at school and eventually kids wonder what all the fuss was about.

Scaffolding is one way to help kids beat their fear. It's all about building up to a situation gently, rather than dropping them in it. If, for instance, your daughter is fearful of going into a new situation on her own, go with her for a short time, then, once she seems settled, find an excuse to leave. Alternatively, support her by spending just a short time at first, then decrease this time as your child gets used to the new environment. Scaffolding beats avoidance and helps overcome fear.

It's always important to validate your child's fears while also letting her know you have faith that she will be able to face them. Point out that she has conquered fear before – when she first rode a bike/gave a talk/slept on her own with the light off – and she can do so again.

Know when to protect, when to support and when to teach

All this talk about risks and fears can make a parent feel quite protective. And that's the point. The instinct to protect – to throw our arms around our children when danger is near or when they are hurting – is strong. It's usually a mother's first response for their sons and daughters. Dads are similarly protective of their daughters but less so with their sons because their instinct is to improve or equip them for the hardships of life. The desire of parents to protect and to keep children safe from harm has served us well over the centuries; our very survival has depended on it.

Protector

But this protective instinct doesn't serve kids well when we over-step the mark and don't allow children to experience the smaller hurts – the scrapes and bruises that go hand in hand with childhood. I'm not just talking about physical scrapes and bruises – curious kids left to their own devices and keen to explore their environments as well as the limits of their own abilities will generally get plenty of those. It's how they learn and it's also how they gain confidence through exploration of both neighbour-hoods and natural environments. Children will also get plenty of emotional bruises, as the social environments they navigate in early childhood and at school can be challenging to say the least. Young children lack appropriate social filters, and despite the best messaging from parents and teachers, can say and at times do some unpleasant things to their peers. Children in primary school and beyond move through a variety of social groups. Some of those groups are a good fit and some are oppressive to those within them, and cruel to those outside them. Navigating the various social environments of childhood for most children means that they'll inevitably be on the receiving end of cruel comments, taunts and teasing and, in some cases, bullying. As a parent you want your kids to breeze through early learning and school without experiencing any of these negative events. You want to protect them – but it's impossible and not always in their best interests.

Supporter

Protector may be an initial default position for many parents when children experience hurt or discomfort, but it's not the only one we can take. There are two stances that are crucial for children's independence and wellbeing – parent as supporter and parent as teacher. Children need parents who can support them emotionally when they experience hardship of any kind – this means that parents need to step back and provide the type of emotional support children need to get by and cope with difficulties. Keeping a child's chin up when life gets hard is one of the most challenging, yet most important, parts of parenting. But it's essential if kids are to develop the strength and fortitude needed to manage some of the social and learning difficulties that will inevitably test them in adolescence and as adults.

Teacher

The education system, which I've been part of for the best part of four decades, has long recognised that parents are children's first teachers. This is in recognition that children develop so much of their language, numeracy and school-readiness skills at home but also that parents teach kids many of the social and emotional skills that are needed to function successfully at school. The teaching role has always been central to effective child-rearing, but it has been devalued as formal education has taken centre stage. In our current Western culture children and young people usually spend less time around their parents than in the past but that doesn't mean the role of teacher should be overlooked. Parents have a huge role to play in teaching kids the skills to get on with each other; as well as the skills to cope with difficulty and hardship. In other chapters in this book I'll further develop the notion of parent as teacher. But for now it's important to acknowledge that moving children from dependence to independence is heavily reliant on parents adopting a teaching role – not necessarily in a didactic way, but willing to help children acquire the skills and experience they need to become confident and self-reliant.

Share the load and the love

Modern parenting is an individual endeavour. We tend to keep all the joys, the frustrations and challenges to ourselves in a way that parents of past generations didn't.

In *Teach your kids to SHRUG!* I wrote about the need to include more 'sparents' – spare parents – in the lives of kids. With the rise of the uber-parent – the parent who does it all, on their own – there has never been a greater need to share the parenting with others, including aunts, uncles, mates and friends.

I wrote that sparents are good for:

- **Filling a gender gap.** If you are raising a son in an all-female household then the regular presence of an uncle, grandfather or male family friend can be the role model that's needed. Similarly, girls in all-male households can benefit from sparenting by a female friend or relative.
- **Filling a talent or interest gap.** Kids usually appreciate having an adult to share their interests, but it's hard for parents to be across all their children's hobbies and activities. Relatives or

family friends can be well placed to fill the interest void that occurs in some families.

- **Babysitting and child-minding.** There is always a need for reliable carers for kids from tots to early teens.
- **Mentoring kids who don't want to listen to their parents.** Teenage boys and girls benefit from having a number of trusted relatives or adult friends in their lives to talk with. Sparents make great confidantes and coaches for young people at a time when they are seeking independence from their parents.
- **Bringing a fresh voice and perspective to kids' lives.** Ever noticed how kids of all ages will listen to other adults more than they listen to their parents, even though the message is the same? It's frustrating, but that has always been the reality of raising children and young people.
- **Doing fun (and costly) things with kids.** Adults without kids usually have more disposable income than parents, placing them in a good position to spoil your kids. Okay, this may be a little trite but there is nothing too much wrong with the occasional splurge from adults who may have a little excess cash to share, particularly when your purse strings are stretched.

In the five years since I penned these words nothing has diminished my belief that child-rearing needs to be a community endeavour. It's central to the redundancy-parenting philosophy. Adults outside a child's immediate family have so much to offer, particularly to a small family.

However, sparenting requires that parents step back and allow others in, and to acknowledge that their way of raising children isn't the only way. There are many ways to be right, so it helps to take in other people's views. It also helps if you allow other people to discipline your child.

Recently, at a children's football game I witnessed the fallout when the coach benched one of his players for unsportsman-like play. During the half-time break he told the boy why he removed him from the field, outlining the behaviour he expected from him in future. The boy's father didn't agree with the coach's assessment of his son and let him know in no uncertain terms. The coach held his ground but he was clearly shaken by the vehemence of the father's approach. As a neutral observer I thought the coach was well within his rights to bench the young player – in fact, he would have been negligent in his duty if he hadn't. The parent's role in this instance was to stand back and support the coach rather than take the side of his child.

Unfortunately, my conversations with teachers and sports coaches suggest that these types of exchanges are increasingly common as many parents are quick off the mark to jump to the defence of their child if they are disciplined in a way that is not to their liking, or for a perceived injustice. It's helpful to remember that schools, sports teams and other groups generally function like large families where those in charge don't always get things right. But children in large families generally understand this and while they may be initially hurt, annoyed or frustrated when they are disciplined they generally learn that the best way forward is to cop it on the chin, learn from the experience and hopefully avoid similar events in the future.

Parents whose aim is their child's independence, and therefore their own redundancy, will generally welcome the input of another adult, particularly in the tricky and challenging area of teaching children to behave well. They also have faith in children's abilities to cope and learn from their experiences so they can adjust their behaviours next time . . . which is what independent kids do.

A big-family mindset: a final word

The hard part about being a grandparent is that I need to stop myself from interfering or giving well-meant parenting advice to my children. It's now their time to bring up kids and find their own parenting way. Of course, like all parents they don't come to the job with a blank slate. They bring with them their own experiences of being parented. If they are like most parents they'll sort through the myriad ways they were raised and cherry pick the methods and ideas that they liked. In effect, they do as food producer John West claims in their promotions – 'take the best and reject the rest'. Great advice, but that doesn't mean that you don't explain to others what your parenting intentions are.

If you adopt the parenting-for-independence philosophy, I suspect that you'll experience doubters and some negativity along the way. You may find that others, including your own family and close friends, will even think you are neglecting your parenting duty if, say, your five-year-old prepares their own breakfast; or your seven-year-old sets their own alarm and wakes themselves up; or that your eleven-year-old has to organise their own transport to an after-school activity because you'll be attending a yoga class at that time. The predominant parenting lens – and the one we tend to look at child-rearing through – is a 'good' parenting lens. Good parents make sure their children are fed. Good parents make sure their children don't watch too much television or spend too much time on various screens. Good parents monitor their children's online activities so that they know at all times what they are up to. Good parents make sure that their children eat nutritious food that maximises their learning potential and ensures they don't become obese. Good parents . . . There's a great deal of pressure to be a good parent, which is magnified if you have a small family of one or two children. The pressure is off when you raise a family of four or more children because you suddenly have a parliament of personalities that you know you can't control; you can only influence them.

The alternative to being a good parent is to become a responsible parent. That is, someone whose aim is to raise kids capable of taking responsibility for their own wellbeing and in effect for their own lives at the earliest possible age. That won't happen in one go. It's a gradual process but essentially it involves giving children responsibility for the many and varied things in their own lives and allowing them to struggle from time to time in the process. And if they aren't ready to take responsibility – say, your five-year-old has to remember to take a book back to school every day as well as their lunch, their bag and other items – then you look for ways – such as giving gentle reminders, or suggesting they place the book in their bag when finished – to make it easier for them to take responsibility. Responsible parents act very differently to good parents, so you need to be ready to be strong and to hold your ground. It's hard to swim against the tide of parenting opinion and I suspect that's what you'll be doing if you adopt the responsible, rather than good, parent code. However it's reassuring to know that being a responsible parent is the short cut to independence and success for your kids. It takes a little parental backbone and persistence to make it happen.

chapter eight

Manage like a cat

Our job as parents is to raise kids so they can be safe; so they can be people-smart; and also so they can adapt to many social situations. As I wrote in Chapter 2 this socialisation process starts when children are young and continues as children's social horizons expand with age. As a general rule this socialisation process is hard work for parents during the preschool years; becomes easier during primary school; and can again be difficult during the adolescent years.

It's also part of our role to develop a sense of responsibility in children. That is, they take responsibility for their behaviour and are not dependent on someone else to rescue them from unpleasant consequences. In effect, they fess up and face up when they have broken a rule, transgressed someone's rights or acted in an anti-social way.

It's not easy being firm

The most difficult, and for some the most unpleasant, part of parenting is dealing with children when they are less than perfect.

For many parents, managing children's behaviour is an incredible struggle. It's fine if you have easy kids or when your kids are in easier stages of development but not so straightforward with those children who don't like to be told what to do; for children and young people who are in defiant or boundary-pushing stages; and for children who have additional needs or medical problems to contend with. That's why parents need a broad repertoire of strategies at their disposal.

In this section I'll introduce a simple but powerful idea for managing kids of all ages. It's related to household pets, so it's easy to follow and remember. Also, this method helps reduce your children's dependency on you and gets you out of the management picture. But first let's look at management and discipline that makes kids dependent on adults, so that we remove these methods from your parenting repertoire.

Discipline that makes kids dependent

There are three behavioural mistakes I see used that may be effective in the short term at either winning kids' cooperation or getting some welcome peace, but they keep kids dependent on parents. No more spoonfeeding disciplinary methods, please!

1. Doing deals with kids

'Jai, if you eat all your dinner up, I'll let you use my iPad for five minutes.' Most kids under the age of ten would empty their plate in an instant with that sort of carrot dangled in their face. But it's a tricky game you play when you start to do deals with kids to elicit cooperation. For a start, you need to be prepared to raise the stakes, because the novelty of five minutes of iPad use will soon wear off. Also, you need to be prepared to keep dealing with your

kids, because they soon learn that if they hang out long enough Mum/Dad/whoever will offer a juicy enticement to win favours.

Do enough deals with kids and they learn that they get what you negotiate. That's fine in the business world, but hard work in families. I've seen mums who do a deal with kids because they just want peace and quickly. I've also seen dads do a deal with their kids because they simply enjoy negotiating. They see it as a game. That's hard work for their partner who doesn't use those methods.

Sometimes it's kids who do the negotiating. *'You want me to go to bed at eight o'clock? Well, I'll go to bed at eight o'clock if I can have a TV in my room,'* says a born negotiator.

It takes a shrewd parent to say, *'Actually, no. That's not going to happen.'* Sometimes we become involved in child-initiated deals before we're even aware it's happening. Again, kids can take advantage of busy, tired or time-poor parents.

Doing deals with kids is one strategy in your armoury to get cooperation from your kids. BUT it needs to be a strategy of last resort (to use when your mother visits; when you are dog-tired; or when you want a cosy Sunday morning in bed), not the first one you use when you want your kids to behave well.

2. Repeating yourself and raising the volume

Ever asked your child for help and been underwhelmed by the response? Or your reminder about bedtime gets no action?

If so, did you repeat your request, as most of us would do? Still ignored?

My bet is that you then tweaked up the volume.

If this routine sounds familiar, your children have a bad dose of parent deafness, an affliction that's becoming increasingly common for many Australian kids. Most kids know how often

Mum and Dad will repeat themselves before they act. They know it may take Mum four times but Dad will go ballistic if they ignore him. They pretty much understand their parents' typical reactions by age four.

If you want to check, just try whispering, 'Anyone for ice cream?' and they'll come running in an instant. Yet a few minutes later ask for help and you'll probably get no reaction. If kids ignore your requests for help you're better off using a consequence or even lowering your voice to get their attention rather than raising your voice or repeating yourself.

3. Using coercion

Some children just like to have their own way. This includes most, but not all, teenagers, and a good many children as well. I'm not sure of the exact figures, but I suspect that about one in three will fit this category. It's not that they are defiant, it's just that control is something they value and they like to feel that they are calling the shots. Use controlling language with these children – 'Do this now!' – and you suddenly have a power play on your hands. They may cooperate with you but they won't go willingly and it will often be done on their terms. 'Want me to clean my teeth? Yeah, in a minute.' Procrastination and last-wordedness is their constant companion when you use coercive language.

Coerciveness is usually accompanied by anger, a raised voice and an icy stare. This simply triggers the fight-or-flight response in their reptilian brain, so they'll either ignore you altogether or they'll start an argument or issue a challenge – *'What do you mean it's my turn to empty the dishwasher? I did it yesterday.'* They may cooperate but it will be through gritted teeth. And you know they'll rely on you to keep reminding them what to do.

Find your inner cat

If you struggle to get your kids to do as you say, it's probably your non-verbals giving you away. That is, it's less about *what* you say, although that does play a part, and more *how* you say it that makes the big difference. If you're not getting cooperation, you are probably managing like a dog, when you should be managing like a cat.

Let's start with dogs. If you have a dog, you'll know it's usually friendly and wants to be shown love and attention. To a dog, you are family. When you feed it it's usually grateful. If it could talk it would say, 'Thank you for feeding me. You're fantastic.' Dogs and dependency go hand in hand.

However, if you own a cat, you'll know that cats are different. They are self-contained and can live happily without you. To a cat, you are staff. If your cat could talk it would probably say when you feed it, *'It's about time. I've been waiting.'* Cats and redundancy go hand in hand.

We all have some cat and dog in us. It's just a matter of access-ing those parts and bringing them out when we need them. The cat is the credible side we all have but find difficult to access. It is always expressed through your non-verbals – that is, your tone of voice, your posture and facial gestures.

A cat speaks with a flat, clipped voice. Her head is very still, her body upright and confident. The quickest way to access your inner cat is to speak with your palms facing the ground. You can try this now. Stand up with both hands in front of you with your palms facing the ground. Now speak. You'll find you naturally speak like a cat – clipped voice, still head and body and more serious expression. This is your credible (and calm) side.

When you speak from your cat side people will usually believe what you have to say. It gives you authority. Australia's foreign minister at the time of writing, Julie Bishop, is a good example. Like her or loathe her, you can't deny she has authority. That's because she accesses the cat side of her nature in public. She is still, uses a flattish, quiet voice and rarely blinks. She looks like she means business.

You manage like a cat by speaking calmly, quietly and staying still. Cats will also withdraw eye contact rather than stand and argue, so look away or respectfully walk away rather than become involved in an argument.

Cats also look for ways to manage visually or kinaesthetically rather than repeat themselves. If they do give an instruction again they are more likely to lower their voice than raise it to get attention. These cat behaviours work well when managing children of all ages, but especially teenagers because most adolescents are cats themselves. Later we'll look at dog behaviours and when to use those. For now I'd like to explore the wonderful world of managing your kids like a cat.

Let the cat out of the bag

Kids need parents who are cats some of the time. Cats who are comfortable with management provide safety to a family. Kids may not always agree with a cat but they will feel safe and comfortable knowing someone is ensuring that there are limits and boundaries and that their rights and wellbeing will be respected. Fairness and fair play is part of young children's DNA and they need to know someone is looking out for them.

Parents who are cat-oriented focus on the family rather than the individual. They look out for the bigger picture and make sure the family as a whole functions well. A mother who makes sure everyone turns up for dinner is bringing her cat to the table.

Similarly, a father acts like a cat when he insists his child apologises for storming off in a tantrum in a game of football and letting his team down.

In this chapter I'll show you how to put some more cat into your parenting, so you can become more effective in managing children's behaviour and gain cooperation, and most importantly make your children less dependent on you. When redundancy is your aim, you need to look for ways to take yourself out of the picture, and reduce children's dependency on you – the best way to do this is to let your cat out of the bag. Here's how.

Manage yourself first

Cats are self-contained and very controlled. So, when you bring some cat into your parenting the first thing you need to do is to learn to manage your own reactions rather than over-react, repeat yourself and just plain yell. I know we get tired and stressed, but fatigue purely reveals our lowest, basest skill level. The trick is to change your thinking. As I wrote in Chapter 5, the biggest struggle for most parents is not the battle they have with children to elicit cooperation but the battle that happens within the grey matter between their ears. It's the battle that goes on between our lizard brain (where the fight-or-flight response occurs) and our pre-frontal cortex (where reasoning and calculation takes place).

The pre-frontal cortex (put your hand on your forehead and you're there) is a cool, calm and rational place. This book is being written from that space. The lizard brain sits way back in the middle of our brain and is programmed to take over from our pre-frontal cortex when we're under threat or stress. If I took a phone call about an imminent bomb threat while in the process of writing, my lizard brain would take over and I'd be out of my office in a heartbeat. Writing would become impossible, not to say stupid! Thank goodness for lizard brain. When I'm safe and feeling calm, my pre-frontal cortex can do its rational thing once more. This system has served us well, keeping us safe for an eternity.

Unfortunately our lizard brain, the simple creature that it is, can't differentiate between a significantly stressful situation such as a bomb threat and an everyday stressor such as a noisy sibling fight that occurs right under our nose. Our limbic system responds in exactly the same way – the lizard brain takes over from our pre-frontal cortex, so you'll either fight (argue, yell, lash out) or flee (get away fast) regardless of the stress. Both situations would elicit the same type of physical response such as an increase in heartbeat, sweaty palms and shortness of breath. Only the severity and intensity of the response is different.

Just when we need to be at our parenting best

So, the great struggle for many parents, and also the great irony, is that when we need to be at our parenting best (when we're responding to poor behaviour or a child's genuine cries for help) our lizard brain often takes over and we're at our parenting worst.

That's why most of us know how we want to respond and communicate with our kids when we're calm but when we are under intense pressure we not only can't find the words we need but we lose our cool as well. Damn that lizard brain!

The good news is your lizard brain can be tricked into working for you, not against you. It takes patience and practice. Here's how.

1. **Recognise the situations and the symptoms**
   Self-knowledge is the best knowledge you can have. When you understand the situations that cause you stress and bring

you quickly to high emotion, you can prepare yourself in advance. Also, when you understand your typical physiological responses you are well positioned to control them. Our physical responses vary. When I'm under intense stress I generally feel nauseous, become physically agitated and my breath gets very high. Knowing this has been a huge help to me staying calm in situations where I used to over-react.

2. **Train yourself to STOP!**

The lizard brain wants you to act fast – to get away, to lash out, to defend yourself – when you're under threat or stress. So, going against this natural urge is a challenge but it can be done. Develop the habit of doing nothing when you find yourself under parenting stress. STOP rather than act impulsively. Don't let the lizard brain win!

3. **Step away and breathe**

Deep nasal breathing is the quickest way to bring down your physical symptoms and rein in negative thoughts that feed your lizard brain. Step away or turn slightly away from the stressful situation to help you breathe slowly and deeply.

4. **Now act!**

Now that your pre-frontal cortex is winning again it's time to think of the best possible response to a tricky parenting situation – which may be to ignore behaviour, use appropriate language or just listen calmly when your child is in distress.

So, how often does your lizard brain win when you experience parenting stress? If it always comes out on top, you'll find it hard to parent as you'd like. You'll be fighting your limbic system as well as your kids. In actual fact you'll manage like a dog and you'll probably end up whining at your kids or else becoming very angry. Get it under control and you'll be better placed to respond to your kids as you'd like to in the cool, calm light of day. That's what cats do.

Cats go low and go near

Watch an experienced teacher or educator in action and you'll notice they rarely raise their voice and they won't repeat themselves unnecessarily to be heard. With more than twenty children to manage over the course of five contact hours each day they'd soon be exhausted if they did so. Rather than raise their voice above the din to be heard, they lower their voice. As I mentioned previously, raising our voice has the effect of making kids ignore us or argue with us. Kids will hear our vehemence but not the detail of our words. By lowering your voice children are more likely to hear you and take notice. They instinctively associate authority with a lower tone of voice, so this works on an unconscious level. Also, the act of speaking in a lower voice means that you have to slow down your breathing, which also places you back in control.

Experienced teachers will also move closer to children to get cooperation rather than bark out orders across the room. In effect they move into the proximal space, about an arm's length away.

Here are two examples.

- A mother at the beach yells at her five-year-old to stop throwing sand. At a distance of ten metres she has little joy. She then moves close to her son, which means she lowers her voice and makes eye contact, and immediately he stops.
- A father shouts out for some help but his two kids ignore his requests as they watch TV. Rather than shout out his instructions again, he goes into the TV room and quietly asks his kids for help. This time he makes a connection and they are far more receptive.

It's not just teachers who can use the Go Low and Go Near principles. They are simple methods to use in family situations to get more cooperation and save yourself the stress and anxiety of continually repeating yourself or raising your voice.

Cats know when to look away

Most people have been trained to make eye contact when they speak. My mother's advice – *'Look at people when you speak to them'* – is still rattling around inside my brain. It's a message that stuck until I met non-verbal communications guru Michael Grinder. An expert in communications, Michael advises parents and teachers to do the opposite; that is, look away from a child when they issue a command rather than look them in the eye. He argues that eye contact at the point of giving an instruction or laying out your expectation is an invitation to an argument. I agree. And it's most valid when communicating with teenagers, who, due to the fact that their brain is being completely rewired, are likely to retreat to their reptilian brain when they feel under threat. So, they'll fight you, ignore you and fly off the handle. That means finger-waving, icy stares and harsh words are out. Instead, use as few words as possible – *'Thomas, clean the kitchen, please,'* rather than, *'Thomas. It's time to clean the kitchen after the mess you've made.'* Keep your voice low and slow and look away, indicating you are not going to argue. And most of the time, but not always, it works. Go cat!

It sounds easy but it takes practice to get right. Recently, I saw a dad invite his three-year-old daughter to go to bed. He said, 'Anna, it's time to come and have a chat about going to bed!' Nothing in his choice of words or his manner indicated he expected his daughter to comply. It was wishful thinking, as she merely sat in the same place watching television. He was managing like a dog. Her mother channelled her best cat, saying in a flat tone, 'Anna,' to get her attention. After making eye contact she then looked away saying, 'Come on, bed!' And she walked toward the bedroom with Anna not far behind. Once they were both in the bedroom her mother gave Anna a big smile and started to chat about the book they were about to read together.

Managing like a cat means using as few words as possible – try to keep it to five words or fewer. Stand strong to indicate control. Keep your voice flat and firm without an inflection at the end. And look away once you've got your child or young person's attention. It's the non-verbals that make all the difference.

Cats don't mix management with relationship-building

If maintaining a strong relationship with your child is a high priority, you need to find a way of separating your management from your counselling and nurturance.

For instance, if a child comes home from school upset about some comments made by a peer but then lets off steam by teasing a sibling, the parents face a dilemma. He has behaved badly by teasing or hurting a sibling, but do you excuse him because he's upset at school? A parent who accesses or channels her cat will quickly manage the situation and address the poor behaviour, because safety is the first priority. Perhaps she'll send him to his room to cool off, or direct him outside to let off steam. This is not the time to talk about the events at school no matter how upsetting they may be. Once the child has calmed down and the tension is removed then it's time to talk about school. Cats are generally very clear about their priorities, which is looking after the wellbeing of their family over the wellbeing of one particular child, regardless of what may have occurred.

Cats use three-point communication

If you've ever accused a teenager of doing the wrong thing, you've probably also experienced some serious teen denial. *'I didn't do it!'* *'I didn't know I had to be home by midnight.'* *'It wasn't my fault. All the others were drinking. I didn't want everyone to think I'm a loser!'*

It can take some pretty tricky communication to get a young person to take your ideas on board, particularly when you want to talk about issues that they don't want to talk about, such as their poor or irresponsible behaviour. But three-point communication works with primary-school kids too, particularly if they deny any wrong-doing.

In a nutshell, three-point communication involves placing the bad news or a representation of the bad news where you can both look at it and discuss it. For instance, if your young person is home late you may both stand in front of a clock and you look at the clock and say, 'We need to talk about you coming home on time.' Looking at the clock rather than at your young person externalises the issue of being late, and gives the young person the chance to reflect and discover for themselves the impact of their behaviour. It also makes it very difficult to argue against. If you are one point, your child a second point, the source of the bad news becomes the third point.

Here are some more examples of using three-point communication with children and young people:

- **Under-age drinking:** Place some alcohol in front of them and point to it saying, *'We need to talk about your drinking.'*

- **A bad school report:** Sit at 90 degrees to your child, place the report down on a table so you can both see it and let your child or young person read it. You both continue to look at the report until your young person wants to talk about how to improve.
- **Broken item:** If you know a child has deliberately broken a toy, piece of furniture or something precious, place the item in front of him, then stand alongside him, point to the item and say: *'Can you help me work out what happened here?'* When your child owns up – they usually do – then it's time to talk about it using two-point communication – that is, make eye contact.

Cats let checklists, charts and help rosters do the managing

We live in an increasingly visual world. A walk down any city street is an assault on your visual sense. There are signs everywhere, of all shapes, sizes and colours competing for your attention.

Our entertainment is increasingly visual. Long ago the television replaced the radio as the number-one family entertainment medium. Now the television has been joined by a wide range of online entertainment options, each highly visual.

Go into most workplaces and there will be messages and signs posted everywhere. Some are motivational (*'If you don't look after your customers our competitors will'*), some are organisational (checklists, daily plans, weekly goals) and some are very personal (pictures of your family, your golf trophy, etc). All are constant reminders of what's important and what needs to be done.

Similarly, schools are full of visual messages and symbols that carry a great deal of meaning for kids. There may be a sign at the school gate with a message to parents and children that usually changes daily. There will be signs on buildings telling kids to 'walk, don't run'; or reminding them of library or sports schedules. Classroom walls are full of charts, lists, graphs and all sorts of visual teaching and memory aids.

Visual management is also applicable to families, although I suspect many parents still rely on their language skills to influence, manage, cajole and persuade their children to behave better and be more responsible at home. In particular, most boys and all kids on the autism spectrum like the constancy and consistency when visual messages and reminders support and reinforce verbal communication.

Checklists and charts

There's nothing like a list or chart to teach kids about daily routines. It doesn't always have to be a parent or sibling that does the reminding when kids need help. A routine in sequential order on a highly visible list or chart is a great learning aid for most kids.

If you are five and just started school, it can be overwhelming trying to get yourself organised each morning. Similarly, if you are easily distracted or have difficulty concentrating, you can forget something, or worse forget the order in which you need to get ready. Checklists are great for teaching children to do jobs or tasks with several parts.

It can be a real help, particularly for organisationally challenged children, to have a list on the back of their bedroom door. A list with, say: 1) Toilet stop, 2) Eat breakfast, 3) Put plates in dishwasher, 4) Get dressed, 5) Pack your school bag, is a simple reminder of the five main activities they need to do to get ready for school each morning.

Photographic charts

A photo chart is another great way to teach a young child to take control of their morning routine. Simply take a photo of your child at each stage of their morning routine and help them place the photos on a chart. Make sure your child is dressed appropriately for each stage, so they learn to associate their clothing with each activity. So, if they have breakfast before dressing for the day, take a photo in their pyjamas, which will help them get things in the right order. Place the photo chart in a public area, or in your child's bedroom.

Help roster

Most parents like the idea of kids helping without being paid but have trouble putting the idea into practice. It can be hard work changing entrenched habits. Besides, you can feel like a nag always reminding kids to help out.

That's why I love rosters. When something needs to be done, refer to the roster. 'Okay, guys, whose turn is it to do the dishwasher?'

It's the humble jobs roster that tells kids what to do, not you. It takes the responsibility of helping right out of your hands. The third party (the roster) becomes the culprit.

There are seven secrets to making rosters rock!

1. **Don't crowd the roster with jobs.** Two to four jobs each day is enough. Not all jobs go on a roster, just the significant ones.
2. **Change the roster each week.** This gives you a chance to rotate the less pleasant jobs.

3. **Place the roster in a public spot.** Accessibility is the key if you are to refer to it often.

4. **Use symbols or simple pictures for non-readers.** Yes, very young children should help.

5. **Make weekends different.** Homes work well when there are two routines. Kids should still help on weekends but differently.

6. **Make a sibling responsible for drawing up the roster** (this can be rotated). This gives ownership to kids.

7. **Include yourself on the roster.** This is the kicker because kids will generally help you if they see that you help them.

Cats use consequences to promote personal responsibility

So, you've served the meal and asked the children to move away from their screens and join you at the table. You've said it nicely. You've also said it firmly. You know that the children have heard you. Besides, you and mealtimes work like clockwork – that the meal is on the table at this time is no surprise to them. So, how long do you wait? How often do you remind kids? As a good parent, believing it's your job to make sure children are fully fed and nourished, you would keep reminding children. You would see it as your responsibility to make sure your children ate their meal.

However, a responsible parent, someone operating from a redundancy mentality, someone who believes kids should be ready to leave home and look after themselves at fifteen, would put the responsibility where it should lie – with children. That would mean you would leave the food on the table for a reasonable amount of time – say, until you have finished your meal – and then remove it from the table.

Cats use consequences, not punishment, to develop social or responsible behaviour. The definition for misbehaviour that cats go by is: *'What does this social situation reasonably require of my child at her age and stage of development?'* In this case, the situation required that her children join her at the meal table to eat. They didn't, so they are indicating they are not hungry. That's a fair and reasonable consequence. Of course, she may have to put up with some pestering, whinging or guilt-laden comments from her brood, but if she's a cat she'll let it wash off her. Maybe she'll even go outside to get away from their attempts to whittle down her will.

Removing the food wasn't the only consequence available to this mother. If eating together was a non-negotiable and her children hadn't joined her after a short amount of time, it would have been reasonable to confiscate the screens, perhaps for the night, because the right children have to use items such as technology, toys, or any item for that matter, is accompanied by a responsibility to stick to some rules of use, and that means ceasing to use them at family dinner time.

All this may sound very logical and practical, but then that is the way of cats. They are pragmatic creatures who abide by rationality and don't let emotion get in the way. They leave that for dogs.

The trick for employing consequences lies in *how* you use them. If you use a consequence with anger, aggression or in a retaliatory way, your children will more than likely be angry at you. However, if you can issue consequences in an impartial, almost nonchalant way – like a cat – your children are more likely to be angry with themselves rather than you.

Being Responsible Chart (Make-up Chart)

One of the great challenges for parents is to teach children to take responsibility for their behaviour. Allowing children to experience the direct consequences of their negative behaviour is one way to develop personal responsibility in kids. A child who is excessively noisy watching TV is asked to leave the room; kids who leave toys around find that someone has collected them and placed them in a hard-to-find spot. Both these consequences teach kids that there is a direct connection between their actions and their outcomes, and so develops a sense of responsibility.

A simple, sometimes fun way to teach kids to take responsibility for their less than desirable behaviour is to introduce them to the notion of a make-up chart. When children's poor behaviour is directed at someone else, such as hurting a sibling or embarrassing a parent in public, they make up for what they've done with a favour or special treat. So, kids who muck up have a chance to make up.

Place a list of make-up behaviours on a chart on the fridge including such treats as: make Mum a cup of tea; give a back rub; set the table; read a story to a younger sibling; empty the dishwasher; do a sibling's jobs for the day.

The make-up behaviours are a form of restitution, so they fit into the category of consequences. Like all consequences they are most effective when delivered calmly so that children are mad at themselves, and are less likely to become defensive.

Manage like a cat – a final word

Many parents feel uncomfortable with the firmer side of parenting, but every family needs a cat because they provide safety – which is essential for children's healthy development. Cats make sure the family functions well and stays on track. Cats also allow dogs to exist and to function well as parents. If two dogs are managing the family, there is a reasonable chance that chaos and disorder will take over. Inconsistency will reign. So, if firmness is a challenge, I urge you to find your inner cat and put it to work at least some of the time. My guess is, your children will appreciate it.

chapter nine

Nurture like a dog

In the previous chapter we looked at cat behaviours and attributes. But that's not the only side we have to our nature. We also have a dog side: the approachable, conversational, relationship-building side. When you access this side you'll speak with a lot of inflection in your voice: your voice will rise and fall and it will sound and feel warmer. Your head will bob up and down too. You'll probably lean forward as you speak and you'll smile a lot – as if you were speaking to a long-lost friend.

The quickest way to access your dog nature is to speak with your palms up. You can try it now. Stand up, put your hands out with your palms up and speak. You should notice a big difference in how you deliver your message from when you spoke with palms facing down. If not, alternate speaking with palms up and down until you see a difference.

The dog side of our nature is what many of us feel more comfortable with. If you hold down a management position in your work then you probably spend more time accessing your cat than your dog; though effective managers will move seamlessly between the two, accessing their dog when networking and relationship-building, and then finding their cat for negotiations or when making decisions.

Actor Hugh Jackman is an example of a public figure who is dog-like – he usually speaks with a lot of cadence in his voice, a big smile and open body language. However, I've seen him switch to cat mode in interviews when he talks about something serious. He will invariably speak quietly, calmly and his head will stay very still. We believe him when he speaks. He's no lightweight. It's his ability to switch from cat to dog and back again that makes him so charismatic.

Children do best when they live in an environment where the significant adults in their life – parents, grandparents and other carers – value them, listen to them, encourage them and nurture them. They also need adults who can place limits, consequences and expectations on their behaviour and manage their behaviour fairly and consistently. This mixture of warmth and firmness, nurturance and expectation is typical of an authoritative style of parenting identified by developmental psychologist Diana Baumrind in the 1960s. Subsequent research consistently supports the view that kids raised under an authoritative parenting model – a balance between tough, austere, parent-centric authoritarian parenting and a laissez-faire, child-centric approach where parents are reluctant to impose rules or standards, known as the permissive parenting approach – are more likely to become independent, self-reliant, socially accepted, academically successful and well behaved. They are less likely to report depression and anxiety, and less likely to engage in antisocial behaviour like delinquency and drug use.

The authoritative approach is a middle ground between the two and tends to be more family-centric than the other approaches. Research suggests that having at least one authoritative parent can make a big difference (Fletcher et al, 1999). Studies consistently report that authoritative parenting is beneficial for kids from a variety of backgrounds and ethnic groups. So, how does this relate to the cat and dog model? A parent's cat-like behaviours and communication techniques provide children with the firmness they need to thrive without the austerity and harshness that so often goes with the authoritarian approach. A parent's dog-like behaviours and communication techniques provide children and young people with the warmth, nurturance and support they need without being smothering or overprotective. In fact, it's the mixture of cat and dog that so impacts raising children of all ages.

Let the dog off the lead

Some people communicate naturally using dog-like gestures and techniques, but it doesn't come naturally to everyone. Anecdotally, many men default to cat behaviour and struggle with the more expressive requirements of dog-like characteristics. Quite simply, many fathers say the words that kids need to hear – *'Well done!'* *'I'm proud of you!' 'Top effort!'* – but their facial expression doesn't quite match the words. In effect, they forgot to tell their face that they were pleased. So, if a toddler has cleaned up her toys without being asked, or your teenager comes home from a party on time, then any words of appreciation uttered need to be accompanied by a big, beaming smile, because that will in all likelihood make a far bigger impression on them than your well-chosen words. Kids are like mood detectives – they're hard-wired to pick up the non-verbals before they pick up your words.

Dogs build relationships through shared activity, fun and play

The cat–dog analogy holds true when it comes to relationship-building. If you've ever played with a cat you'll know that it mainly involves teasing. You'll tease their interest by rolling a ball their way, or dangling a piece of string in front of them; it's all one-way – their way. When they lose interest they stop, rarely giving anything back. On the other hand, play a game with your dog – note, you may have to choose your breeds carefully – and play is generally more two-way. They'll bring that ball back to you; they'll nudge you and maybe they'll even lick your hand or your face in a display of affection. So, what can our canine and feline friends teach parents about building relationships with children?

I think the big lesson a dog teaches us is the absolute need for parents – both mothers and fathers – to engage with their children in playful ways. We underestimate the place of fun and playfulness in parenting. These are times when we let our guards down as adults and let our children get close to us. Fathers have traditionally used play and games as a way to get closer to their offspring. In my book *A Man's Guide to Raising Kids* I wrote that the language of fathering was a physical one and involved a great deal of play. I also discussed the benefits of rough play, a horizontal, no-holds-barred wrestling match between dads and their under-fives that not only taught kids emotional restraint but was a brilliant way for men to get close to their kids both physically and emotionally. Of all the ideas and concepts discussed in this book the notion of rough play received the strongest reaction from fathers. Yet, since penning that book fifteen years ago it's my observation that rough play seems to be on the wane. The reasons are unclear, but it does coincide with the rise in the age of fathers – the average age of first-time dads is now over thirty – and the fact that many dads work longer hours than ever.

In my book *Working Parents* I wrote about the value of one-on-one time for parents to build strong relationships with children. One-on-one time refers to the opportunities parents take to spend time alone with their children in a pleasurable or fun activity ranging from shopping together, reading a story, talking, using technology or even playing a game on a mobile device. But one-on-one time only works as a relationship-builder if you approach it in the same manner a dog approaches a game – with readiness to engage and a determination to hold nothing back. Approach the activity like a cat – begrudgingly and not whole-heartedly – and the chances are it will end in tears as you'll more than likely argue because you won't be in the right mood; alternatively, your child will become bored when you fail to enter into the spirit of things.

Dogs increase good feelings at home

Strong families thrive on good feelings. That doesn't mean that such families are devoid of conflict or criticism, but that they are generally pleasant environments to be part of. One way to increase good feelings in your family is to increase the number of compliments kids hear at home.

As a general rule, the ratio of compliments to criticism should be around five to one. That is, there should be five times more positive, affirming comments than negative comments.

In unhealthy families this ratio is often reversed. Five negative comments for every one positive comment makes for a toxic environment.

How does your family rate on this scale?

If you think about how your family might rate on this scale, be careful how much weight you put on your children's comments, especially to each other. Siblings can be unkind to each other, finding it hard to share a pleasant word, which can skew the positive-to-negative ratio a lot (and sometimes make family life awful for everyone).

However, this can change over time.

Here are five ideas to help you improve the compliments-to-criticism ratio in your family.

1. **Increase the number of affirmations and compliments *you* make.** These, along with affectionate phrases and kind remarks, will start to skew the ratio. Aim for a seven-to-one ratio. Not only is this good modelling for your kids, but it will make family life more harmonious.
2. **Keep a check on your use of good-feeling killers (and self-esteem killers).** Eradicate comments such as: *'Typical boy!' 'If I've told you once I've told you a thousand times, don't . . .' 'What a stupid thing to say to your brother/sister!'* Bite your tongue. If you find yourself thinking a criticism, keep it to yourself.
3. **Make kids aware of their language** and the potential harm to self-esteem, not to mention family harmony, that constant criticism can cause. Use 'I' statements to let kids understand the impact their negative talk has on you. *'When you talk so aggressively I feel quite scared about what you are going to do next.'* It's impossible for kids to disagree with 'I' statements.
4. **Make it a habit to follow a negative with a positive.** When I was teaching I always tried to follow discipline of a student with a compliment or some positive feedback so that we could

maintain a good relationship. Do the same in your family. Follow discipline, a rebuke or a negative comment with a positive act or comment. Then teach your kids to do the same.

5. **Let the bad feelings out.** Sometimes there can be such a build-up of ill will between siblings that you need to find a way for them to let the bad feelings out. One way to do this is to let one child vent to you about their sibling. Be warned that you may not like what you hear, but a clearing of the air can work wonders to improve the family atmosphere.

Most of these suggestions start with you, the parent. Like everything in family life, whatever you want from your kids, you must take the lead and do first. Remember, five positives to one negative is your aim.

Dogs listen attentively to their children but they don't always act on what they say

One of the most difficult things for a time-poor parent is to listen to children when they have problems. You know the drill. A four-year-old runs to you with a tale of woe about his bigger sister – '*She won't give me back my &&&&. She says I gave it to her and I never did.*' A six-year-old comes home from school complaining about her best friend – '*She's being mean to me. She won't play with me any more.*' A ten-year-old laments the fact that he just missed being picked for the school football team – '*It's just not fair. I'm a better player than Jeremy, but he gets a game.*' A thirteen-year-old has just had a disagreement with a teacher that he doesn't feel is just – '*That teacher always picks on me, but this time he went too far.*' These types of situations challenge the judgement and goodwill of any well-meaning parent. Should I listen?

Should I brush it off? Should I intercede on my child's behalf? Let's look a little closer.

We all need to share our story with someone when we feel upset or angry – children are no different to adults in that regard. Perhaps the difference is that some children don't see the full picture, so they can easily misinterpret events, and underestimate their place in the scenario or overestimate the place of others. Also children, like some adults, can easily exaggerate a situation. 'This is the worst thing ever!' rather than 'That was unpleasant.' 'Everyone hates me!' rather than 'There are kids in my class I don't get on with.' This means as parents we need to listen to our children when they have difficulty; but we don't always have to resolve their problem. Rather, we can help them give voice to their frustrations and difficulties so that they can work through their emotions and also see a situation a little more rationally. 'I understand how you must feel' is perhaps the most important thing you can convey to a child or teenager when they genuinely feel hurt or aggrieved.

Sometimes as parents we need to act on our children's behalf. We need to be their advocate and speak to a sibling about their behaviour or arrange an appointment with a teacher to talk about friendship or other issues that may need to be raised on your behalf. That's when the dog behaviours stop and you need to switch to cat behaviours. Remember, cats are calm; they stick to the facts; they have strong body language and a firm voice. Avoid speaking to a child or addressing professionals at preschool or school with anger and aggression; children and teachers may well placate you, or give you space, but the chances are you'll be completely ineffective in acting in the best interests of your child. They'll treat you and perceive you in the same way as they would an angry dog, which matches the behaviours you . are exhibiting.

So, when you listen go dog, when you act on their behalf switch to cat.

Nurture like a dog – a final word

Just as some breeds are friendly and more approachable than others, parents will differ in their demonstrativeness to their kids. Some parents have big smiles and use big gestures when they are happy, while others will use smaller gestures and be more restrictive in their movements. The important thing is that you display dog behaviours that are different to cat behaviours. You don't need big gestures and variations to be a dog – they just need to be different to your cat. It's these differences that your kids will pick up.

chapter ten

Bring some cat *and* dog to your parenting

Effective parents nuance their communication. That is, they alter their style to suit the situation rather than let their moods dictate their communication style. This is not necessarily conscious; however, do it often enough and switching from cat to dog and back again becomes a habit.

My challenge for you is to bring your cat to the table when you want to manage children's and teenagers' behaviours, and access your dog side when you encourage them, build relationships and listen to them.

Get your cat and dog wrong and you'll be ineffective. Manage like a dog and you'll do one of three things: 1. Whine at your kids, 2. Use an angry voice, 3. Do nothing because you don't want to offend them. Build relationships like a cat and you'll be distant, stiff and unapproachable. Get the mix right and you'll be able to give your children exactly what they need. That is, the leadership and safety that cats provide and the nurturance and encouragement that comes naturally to dogs.

So, does the cat side or the dog side come more naturally to you? Think about it. When you discover what you default to, you need to be aware of two things. First, you will need to work a little harder to access the other side. Second, make sure you don't rely on one side of your nature to do the work in your communications with your children. If you do, you will more than likely either manage or nurture well but rarely do both well. However, get the mix right and you'll have discovered the key to charismatic parenting and leadership.

Manage like a cat, nurture like a dog. Who would have thought it's that simple?

Warm dog, firm cat

Partners who work well together as parents often share the roles of cat and dog; it's a family variation of the infamous good-cop–bad-cop routine. It's not that they deliberately set out to play particular roles, but usually one parent will by default be either the firm or the warm parent, leaving their partner to assume the other role. This natural preference is usually determined by personality, our own experience of being parented and our beliefs about child-rearing.

The gender of both parents and child plays a part when it comes to the cat and dog roles parents take. Many fathers are very firm with their sons, always driving them to achieve and do more. They frequently expect them to put in a great deal of effort in any endeavour that they tackle and at times can be overly tough and unforgiving when their sons don't meet their lofty standards. Many mothers, on the other hand, offer their sons the warmth and nurturance they need, the counterbalance if their father is too firm.

On the other hand, many fathers are like puppy dogs in the hands of their daughters because they have vastly different expectations about their behaviour. Youngest daughters almost always have their father wrapped around their little finger.

Many mothers have difficulty being the firm cat when they parent their sons, particularly their youngest son who so often stays a baby for life. Yet these same mums can be extremely cat-like when they parent their daughters, especially when their youngsters make the transition to adolescence.

The firm-cat, warm-dog roles fit the authoritative parenting framework that serves children so well, with one parent compensating for the shortfall or perceived failings of the other.

Cat and dog is situational

Some situations require parents to be cat-like while others require the dog to take over. It's apparent to parents of preschool and early primary school children that transition times in families are one of the most difficult times for parents to manage. The type of parenting approach used can make a huge difference at these pivotal parts of the day.

Cats take over from dogs in transition times

Those transition times in families – when children move from one activity to another; from playing a game on their own to being in the car; from having fun to joining the family for dinner; from enjoying a game to going to bed – are challenging for many parents. These are the situations when children are most likely to procrastinate, argue and resist. Dog-like parents will invariably remind their kids to cooperate and to hurry along when kids drag the chain. Some will become whiny dogs making comments like, *'Come on, you know you should be going to bed. You don't need me to remind you. Just clean your teeth and go to bed, would you!'* The alternative tends to be the angry dog that barks out instructions. *'How many times do I have to tell you! Move it! Now!'* Either way, children remain dependent on their parents when they channel their inner dog during these times of transition.

Cats, however, take a different approach. The whole aim of redundancy parenting is to make children less dependent on their parents. That means children self-govern or take responsibility for their behaviours, especially around transition times. It's fascinating to note that parents in large families generally don't report the same level of discontent with transition times as parents of smaller families. I suspect that this may be for a couple of reasons. First, siblings in larger families tend to take over many parenting roles, managing the movements of children at those traditionally difficult times of the day such as getting up and getting off to preschool or school; transitioning to the evening meal or managing bed-times. Second, in the absence of siblings as surrogates, parents have less time and propensity to involve themselves with children during transition times. They may, for example, simply get ready to drive the car to school in the morning rather than hang about the house rounding up dawdlers. In the absence of a dog to round them up, most children will make their way to the car on time . . . well, nearly on time.

There are a number of ways a cat will approach transition times. These include the following.

Cats cue rather than continually remind

Cats are self-contained and so they don't wish to continually remind others to cooperate or move to the next activity. They do, however, understand that some children need assistance to transition – so they may use a timer to let toddlers know when it's time to pack up. Primary-school children should know in advance when it's bedtime so they can be prompted to keep an eye on the clock. Alternatively, key times such as bedtime can be anchored to other activities such as going to bed at the end of a particular program. Cats will invariably be on the lookout for strategies that make it easy for children to remember their responsibilities, including sticking to normal household routines rather than constantly reminding them and taking the responsibility away.

Cats consistently stick to routines

Above all else children love routine – those step-by-step predictable processes we put in place that make family life simple and easy to follow. Some children may fight the restrictive nature of routines, but this is natural in many ways. Routines provide children with the type of structure they need to feel like they are in control – and children crave control. Cats stick to routines and don't cave in when children push against the boundaries. They stand their ground, or, even better, make themselves scarce during transition times so kids can't argue or pester them to change their mind.

Cats use consequences to teach

Dogs are naturally noisy, so they'll almost always use their voice to get more cooperation. Like sheep dogs who yap at the heels

185

of wandering sheep, some parents will continually harangue, remind or chastise their children to elicit cooperation. Cats rarely make a sound at the point of conflict, preferring to scratch or inflict something unpleasant. Well, as parents we don't need to resort to physical means when children drag the chain or try to keep us involved during these times of transition; however, we can use logical or natural consequences to encourage children to self-manage more at these times. So, procrastinating kids can go to school without breakfast in the morning; latecomers will miss bedtime stories; and toys not packed away can be removed by the silent robot overnight and withheld for a few days. Cats also deliver consequences calmly and nonchalantly, indicating to children that they won't get involved in arguments.

Cats don't allow their moods to dictate their reactions

Dogs allow their moods to dictate the way they manage children. When they feel good, routines go out the window and kids get away with a great deal. When they feel bad, stressed or over-tired, they come down heavily on their children. This inconsistency leads to resentment and further lack of cooperation. Cats are more objective, and while they recognise their moods change, they fundamentally won't change much about their expectations and management of their family. One way to stop your moods dictating your management style is to stick to known rules, limits and boundaries rather than be overly flexible and generous in your interpretation when you are in a good mood. Consistency is one of the greatest gifts you can give your children, because it generally ensures the type of predictability they need for healthy development.

Cat and dog is developmental

The developmental nature of childhood means that they are constantly changing physically, cognitively and emotionally. These changes mean that parents need to adapt their styles to meet their children's changing needs.

Infancy

If you have a baby, you need to provide a great deal of emotional support, warmth and nurturance. There is no doubt a baby will quickly bring out the inner dog in most people. However, there are times, such as when you need to reassure rather than nurse a wakeful baby, that you need to call on your inner cat – which is quiet, unemotional and calm – so that he will return quickly to sleep. Yes, even babies need to be managed at times.

Toddlers to preschool aged

Toddlers usually have a way of helping parents find their inner cat, whether it's through frenzied activity, a determination to have their own way or a refusal to cooperate with your agenda. It's during this stage that you need to mix firmness with warmth but, just as you do when raising teenagers, you may need to err on the side of catness more than you feel comfortable with.

Primary-school aged

Kids in latency (the primary school years) are generally easier to manage, and due to their outward orientation to the world they need a great deal of assistance and support to help them negotiate the many social situations that they experience, whether it's new after-school activities, mixing with adults or making friends at school. As parents you generally find yourself doing a great deal of relational work with your kids during this stage, which requires you to bring more dog to your interactions.

Adolescence

Teenagers need a mix of firmness and nurturance from their parents. Like toddlers, many teenagers wear L plates when it comes to navigating their expanding world. Of course, the world a teenager inhabits is far broader than that of a toddler, so the risks are multiplied a hundredfold. They still need to be managed, but not necessarily in controlling or confrontational ways.

Due to physiological changes most teens will revert straight to their reptilian brain when they feel threatened or experience angry, aggressive discipline. They will fight you all the way, or escape conflict by going to their room or withdrawing into themselves. Better to manage like a cat so they hear your message rather than pick up your vehemence.

Making cat and dog work for me

From a personal perspective, I'm far more cat than dog. Like many cat-like people I can be quite critical of others and quite reserved in my relationships. I'm not overt with affection, but rather thoughtful and self-contained. I naturally default to being the firmer parent. It's not that I can't be affectionate, encouraging or build strong relationships, I just need to work a little harder than my wife, Sue, who naturally exhibits dog-like behaviours. She has always been the relationship-builder in our family, and like many dogs she is naturally encouraging, but she also knows how to be cat when the need arises.

It helped to know my natural preference and what that entails. It means that I'd consciously ask myself when I was with my children – 'What does this situation require of me?' If my child was upset about something, I needed to be more dog-like in my approach, be willing to listen rather than direct or instruct. That meant I had to stop what I was doing, make eye contact (dogs always make eye contact), adopt a friendly tone of voice and also sit so we'd be on the same level. If a decision needed to be made or instruction given, I needed to be more cat-like. That is, use strong body language, use a firm voice and, of course, use a minimum of words to get my point across. There are times when the no-nonsense approach of cats is absolutely the best approach to take in family situations. I found that, with practice, dog-like parenting behaviours became more natural to me, so I was able to become the more rounded, flexible parent that my children needed me to be.

Parenting solo – cat and dog

The hardest part for parents who raise their kids on their own is not so much that they have to do the myriad parenting jobs themselves; by far the most challenging part is that you have to play both the role of firm cat and warm dog – usually simultaneously. It's not just single-parent-led families where solo parenting occurs. Many intact families are led by a solo parent because one parent, more likely to be the father, works away from home for significant periods or else lives at home but keeps their parenting participation to a minimum. From observation those solo parents who are most successful have a full understanding of when they need to be firm and when warmth is called for. Put it another way: they know when to be cat-like and when to be dog-like with their children, and they don't let guilt stand in the way of doing what needs to be done. The cat/dog framework is a practical way for sole parents to offer their children the type of parenting they need to suit different situations.

Bring some cat *and* dog to your parenting – a final word

Your ability to switch between cat and dog will impact your effectiveness as a parent. Many parents, indeed many people, switch automatically and unconsciously between firmness and friendliness. Those people are naturally charismatic. It's my experience that you can consciously switch between the two modes but it takes both awareness and practice. It's best to understand what comes easiest for you – in my case, cat is easiest for me to access and be conscious of when the other side is required. Personally, I have to put some effort into being more dog-like – I remind myself that my face should light up, I need some inflection in my voice and that I should make solid eye contact when I'm giving a compliment. That's my battle. You may do the dog-like behaviours easily but have to work a little harder at the cat behaviours when you need to manage and be firmer with your kids. In time these transitions become automatic as we take on new habits and new ways of working with our kids.

part four

RAISE independent kids at each stage

So far we've looked at the characteristics of resilience, account-ability, integrity, self-confidence and emotional intelligence – the things parents should focus on when raising kids to become independent and self-reliant. Then we looked at how parents can develop a big-family mindset, and how managing like a cat and nurturing like a dog can help you bring independence-building to life. Now it's time to investigate some more practical ways to develop independence during each major stage of development – in early childhood, latency (primary-school years) and adolescence. In this section you will find practical ideas and strategies to help you promote resilience, accountability, integrity, self-confidence and emotional intelligence at each stage. Keep in mind that these are suggestions and that the strategies aren't contained to any particular stage, but may be used at different ages depending on individual children and circumstances.

chapter eleven

Age two to five –
The independent years

A snapshot of this stage

This early stage of life is a time when children like to copy the adults around them. Their most important relationships are with members of their family. They enjoy playing with other children, although some of this play will be alongside others rather than with them. It is a time when kids develop the independence and social skills they will use for learning and getting on with others at school. In this period, parents can develop self-help skills in their children such as dressing themselves, preparing simple meals and packing toys away.

During this stage children get an understanding of their gender and may show a preference for playmates of their own sex. Some children may have difficulty separating from their parents early in this stage but this should become easier with age.

In this age group, children can be easily frustrated as they learn to better express themselves and regulate their emotions. You can help them cope with these strange feelings by describing back to them how they might be feeling. This lets them know that they are being understood and helps them develop the words they need to calm themselves down. You can also help your child to regulate their emotions by being calm yourself, and giving them the tools and language needed to change the way they feel.

Children in this stage are very curious about the world, so expect to answer a wide range of questions. It's an age when kids should spend a great deal of time with other children in their neighbourhood and in the broader world. It's also a time when parents can teach children good manners, ways to interact with other children and how they can be helpful.

Preschoolers use their growing vocabulary to increasingly express feelings, ideas and curiosity about the world around them. Make sure you spend plenty of one-on-one time with them to build this vocabulary and their communication skills.

Independence

Recently I arrived in the afternoon at the venue where I was presenting to parents that night. I was met by a mother and her three-year-old daughter who insisted she would carry my laptop bag into the hall for me.

'I'll carry that!' she said.

Who was I to argue? She struggled with it for a good minute or so before giving it back to me. 'There you are. You can carry it now!' It was clearly too heavy but she had a smile on her face as she raced off to play with a friend.

Harness the helping habit

Miss 3, like most children around her age, is primed for independence. She wanted to help; to feel useful. So, it's the stage to harness all this enthusiasm and develop the helping habit in children. Soon she'll move into a different stage and will be too busy with other interests to help. Of course, this means that we need to slow down and go at their pace to allow this habit to develop. At this stage you need to add an extra few minutes to every interaction you have with a toddler or young child to enable them to help. Unfortunately, many parents lack the time needed to facilitate this helping habit in very young children. Usually we just want to get things done, so it's easier to do a job ourselves – whether it's undressing a toddler, tidying toys away or smoothing the doona on a bed – rather than give young children the opportunity to complete these jobs themselves.

It's during early childhood that parents can begin to instil the helping habit so that it becomes the baseline to build on during childhood and adolescence. Rarely have I met an independent adolescent who didn't have independence and usefulness drummed into them from an early age. So, the key to long-lasting independence-building is to start in early childhood.

Do things together

The best way to teach kids the skills and attitudes for independent living at this age is to do things together. Again, this can be time-consuming for parents, but the time spent together will pay future dividends in terms of the skills learned and a healthy relationship.

Invite children to help

Recently I spent some time with a mother of three children under the age of five who was training her tribe to be useful. She spent a great deal of her time directing children to either help her or perform simple tasks for themselves. *'Cassie, can you get me your blue T-shirt from your bottom drawer?' 'Ella, please put this towel in the bathroom for me.' 'Cassie, help Timothy put his dirty cup in the sink.'* This was not just about keeping kids busy, but training her kids in the fine art of being helpful.

Resilience

Children during this developmental stage are busy forming strong attachments to the central figures in their lives – family and carers. These attachments give them the confidence to explore the world in the knowledge that there is someone to reach out to when they need assistance. These attachments are also central to the development of resilience in young children. Feeling accepted and loved helps children get through the hard times they may experience.

During early childhood there are many practical ways you can build the foundation for future resilience as well as assist them to manage some of their frustrations, difficulties and challenges. Let's look at a few.

Praise persistence

Some young children get frustrated by their inability to complete simple tasks and can easily give up. But this is the age when persistence should be encouraged. *'Come on, keep going. You'll get there. You just need to be a little patient.'* Comments such as this link success to effort and reinforce the notion that patience, effort and persistence are virtues even at this young age.

Take their worries seriously

Early childhood is a time when anxieties and worries become very real. Children under the age of five view the world through a slightly different lens to adults. The part of the brain that rules rational thinking isn't quite developed yet, so they fear things adults see as rational. Fear of separation from significant adults, fear of the dark, fear of spiders and bad things happening to them are common. Help children of this age control a worry by giving it a name – it makes it feel less scary and more manageable. My favourite picture storybook for toddlers, *There's a Hippopotamus on our Roof Eating Cake* by Hazel Edwards, personifies fear of the dark as a friendly hippo. Much friendlier and easier for a child to boss around.

Model optimistic thinking

American psychologist Martin Seligman, in his research conducted more than two decades ago, informed us of what we all know: kids are natural copycats. He found that children have a natural tendency to copy their primary parent's explanatory style. They tended to approach problems and challenges with similar self-talk and mindsets as the parent they spend most time around, or a parent they admire most. Optimism is one of the four attributes that resilient people share (the others are independence, social connection and problem-solving skills) and as Seligman's work shows, optimism is developed in the early years. Early childhood is the time to model optimistic thinking if you want your kids to develop glass-half-full rather than glass-half-empty thinking.

Teach children to wait

Patience, impulse control and delayed gratification are important attributes for kids to develop if they are to succeed both socially and academically at school. The best way to promote these attributes at this stage is to encourage kids to wait – wait your turn; wait until the big hand is on twelve before you get up from the meal table; wait until your birthday in a week's time to get that toy.

Here are some simple ideas to help young children learn to wait.

1. Teach them little rhymes, such as: *'Count to eight, it helps me wait: 1-2-3-4-5-6-7-8!'* Ask them to say it with you. Rhymes, chants and songs help children focus their attention on something else while they wait.
2. Put routines in place that help children practise waiting. For example, give them something regular to look forward to, such as seeing their grandparents at the end of the week.
3. Praise your children for waiting. *'It's hard to wait to play with your cousin, but you did it! You are learning how to wait calmly for things you want!'*

Teach children to ask for help

Early childhood is the ideal time to teach children how they can ask for assistance when they experience difficulty. Start by encouraging them in everyday conversations to ask for what they want rather than whining or merely pointing. Help them find the words to verbalise their wishes. Then discuss with them the people to whom they can go to talk about their worries as well as how they might approach others. It's useful to give them a line or word to use that may trigger the other person to listen to them.

Accountability

The move from infancy, where babies are very dependent on parents, to early childhood, where children develop a real sense of independence, is a challenging time for parents. It's a move from a time of soft love (infancy) to firm love (early childhood) where you are managing a young child who may be physically very able but who hasn't the maturity to match. Children in the two-to-three-year age group generally present the most challenges to parents until adolescence arrives and then more complex challenges emerge.

Children in early childhood need to learn to be social and also that they can't have everything their own way or always get what they want. This is the stage when parents, if they haven't already, find their inner cat. That is, the side of them that is less worried about relationship-building and nurturance and more concerned with providing children with the safety and consistent environment needed for them to stay safe and be more social as their world expands.

This age group benefits from boundaries and routines to guide their behaviour. Both add certainty and a measure of control to their activities. Establish routines for mornings, the evening rush hour, mealtimes and bedtime. (There are lots of ideas about establishing routines in my book *Great Ideas for Tired Parents*.)

Behaviour management strategies suitable for this stage include the following.

Reminders about good behaviours

Children at this age wear L plates when it comes to being social, so plenty of reminders about good behaviour help. Your child will benefit from little reminders about how they should speak to others, how to behave with other children and how to act with adults.

Removal: time in and time out

As cute and as loveable as toddlers and preschoolers can be, there are times when they just get under our skin as parents and carers, as well as under the skin of peers and siblings. Sometimes they can lose control and throw a giant tantrum because they don't get their own way. At other times they may annoy a family with continuous noisy or unsociable behaviour to such an extent that you feel that you'll just about do anything to make the behaviour stop. At those times children may need to be removed from the situation and placed into either 'time out' (often in another room) or 'time in' (near the parent) to break a pattern of poor behaviour or in some situations to give children a chance to reflect on what they may have done and think about more appropriate ways of behaving. When done calmly and respectfully, removing your child is an effective way to help them become social and safe to be around. They can go to a safe place such as their bedroom or to a quiet place near you. It's important that calm is restored and that they are ready to rejoin the human race and behave appropriately.

Behaviour rehearsal

Children in this age group love to role play and can really benefit from practising a whole range of pro-social behaviours that will prepare them for new situations. Want them to stay in bed if they wake up in the middle of the night rather than get up and come into your room? If so, role play waking up and turning on the light and looking at some books rather than coming to your room. Want them to use their best manners when they go to other children's homes? If so, encourage them to use their best manners around the meal table at home, using dolls and toys instead of people. Behaviour rehearsal is a wonderful way of imprinting social and sociable behaviours on this impressionable age group.

Stay close

Some younger children need their parents to be close to them in social situations to calm them down and coach them on how to interact with others. *'It's not your turn to blow out the candles, Alex. Leave it to the birthday boy!'* Lots of coaching at this stage is useful.

Introduce logical consequences

This is a stage during which children can gradually be introduced to logical consequences. It's important to do this in a firm, fair and forgiving way. Removal is the most effective consequence for children of this age – whether it's removing a child from a difficult situation, removing a toy that they are hurting someone with or removal of the right to be in an area or room. Consequences are most effective when they are accompanied by an explanation of what the child has done and what they should do next time. Sometimes the explanation can come after the event that led to a consequence, particularly if a child is emotional or upset.

Use natural consequences, except when their safety is concerned

There will also be times that nature and natural circumstances can teach your child to be responsible and autonomous. For example, when a child puts his shoes on the wrong foot the discomfort he feels may teach him the right way to wear shoes.

Integrity

During this stage a child's social circle is small and your influence as a parent is large. Integrity development needs to occur primarily within the family context – and needs to be couched in terms of doing the right thing by others. This includes helping young children play and get along with both younger and older siblings and make social connections with other children. Girls often have a head start because their brain is more acutely wired for socialising at this age than that of boys. For instance, four-year-old girls who meet each other for the first time are likely to find out each other's name and begin a game without outside prompting. Boys, on the other hand, at the same age, are more likely to play side-by-side and less likely to learn each other's names. So, boys generally need more coaching and coaxing at this age to be social.

During the early years adherence to good manners and the encouragement of helping behaviours are the best ways to promote a sense of integrity. Teaching and positive recognition are a parent's main tools. Teach children the language of manners from an early age. Focus on the big three – 'please', 'thank you' and 'excuse me' – from a young age in a variety of situations. For instance, when a three-year-old wants something, remind him to say please; alternatively, give him what he wants but remind him to say 'please' next time. For four-year-olds and beyond it's appropriate to remind them before they go out in public that they should use manners when they are with other people, which is the true test of whether your teaching has worked.

Give young children the chance to help you in simple everyday situations such as when you are shopping, cooking or cleaning the house. Expecting children to offer assistance at this age normalises helpfulness and capitalises on young children's natural wish to be useful.

Self-confidence

In the two-to-five-year age group, children are already beginning to separate themselves physically and emotionally from their parents. They learn about themselves in fairly physical ways, and will begin to compare themselves to others. Parents need to mirror back to children in this age group that they are capable, while also offering a safe, secure and stable environment for them to explore and develop their capabilities.

Children in this age group generally respond strongly to praise. They often have difficulty distinguishing between *what they do* and *who they are*, so when you praise their efforts or performance, they see you praising them. Their self-esteem is linked to how you feel about their behaviours. Consequently, kids in this stage often prefer praise over encouragement. They will usually respond very well to 'descriptive praise' that tells them about their behaviour. *'You've packed your toys up straightaway after you finished with them. I love the way you keep your toys tidy.'*

Try the following practical confidence-building strategies.

Spend enjoyable one-on-one time with your child every day

Never underestimate the value of spending individual time with a child. It builds rapport and a sense of self-worth.

203

Provide simple choices to increase personal power

Give young children some measure of control over clothing choices, the types of food they eat and how they can contribute to the running of the house. Avoid providing children with a smorgasbord of choices, particularly when it comes to choosing food. Instead, offer a choice between two or three items. 'What should we cook for dinner tonight? I was thinking either pasta or fish. What do you think?' This type of active involvement is a great way to show kids you value them.

Encourage confidence through play

When children play they can take the time they need to master activities that interest them. This builds confidence and motivation to try new things. Playing also promotes development of flexible thinking and creative problem-solving skills. It's through free play that children feel a degree of control over their environment. It's also how they practise and learn many of their social skills. This age group will frequently mimic their parents' language during imaginative play sessions, which can be a little daunting indeed.

Set children up for success

Encourage them to do a task one step at a time. This helps children see their progress step-by-step and motivates them to keep trying. Give them things to do that they are capable of but that also challenge them to gently stretch their abilities and learn something new. This helps them tolerate small amounts of 'healthy' stress and shows them that effort is needed to learn new things and solve problems. It also helps them learn to deal with frustrations in daily life.

Emotional intelligence

Self-control and self-regulation are the building blocks of emotional intelligence at this age and stage of development. Self-control is an inner strength that plays an important part in developing self-regulation, which is our ability to adjust our feelings, thoughts and actions to suit different situations. If you have ever been overwhelmed by big emotions such as anger, annoyance or extreme anxiety, you'll know how hard self-regulation can be. But self-regulation helps kids handle life's disappointments, worries and frustrations without becoming overwhelmed by them.

Self-regulation starts with breathing

Deep breathing is the pathway to calm. It's something that every adult can practise and learn and it's a skill that we can easily teach young children. Deep belly breathing is best practised in fun, no-stress situations.

Help young children regulate their thinking

Teach young children to think pleasant thoughts when they are scared or upset, and so learn to calm themselves down. Help your child to picture something pleasant (like a favourite animal or a special place). Alternatively, you can help them identify a happy place to go when they want to feel happier. It may be a bedroom, a favourite chair or little cubby under a blanket that they have built where they feel safe and comfortable.

Help them feel comfortable with strong feelings

Let children know that while strong feelings are permissible, certain behaviours aren't okay. Help young children express their feelings with words when they're upset. Use language such as, *'We don't hit when someone takes our things. Tell Max that you are mad. Let him know that you'd like your ball back.'*

chapter twelve

Age five to ten –
The competency years

A snapshot of this stage

This is a stage of life known as 'latency', where children have the task of gaining a sense of competency. It's the stage where they begin school and start to form relationships with adults and children outside their family.

It's a time of enormous learning, where they begin to read, write, undertake maths and do many other school-based tasks. Children in this stage are also learning a great deal about their own capabilities and are starting to form a picture of themselves and how they fit into the different groups they belong to.

During this period, children often become increasingly busy with outside-school activities. They discover their strengths and develop interests that may well stay for life. Traditionally this has been a generalist stage in which children explore many different types of activities that will then tend to be whittled down to a few core interests in adolescence.

This is the stage for parents to develop processes of communication with their children that will take them into adolescence. It's also the time to develop good health and wellbeing habits ahead of adolescence, particularly around sleep. Lack of sleep during adolescence can be a significant problem.

In these years parents build on the independence skills that were initiated in early childhood so that children see themselves as capable. Children at this age should be taught many of the skills needed for independent living such as how to prepare food, how to work out a schedule and how to ask adults for help. It's a good idea to add extra time to your schedule each day to teach children self-help skills and also to be available to talk about school.

Although children in this stage spend a great deal of time at school or among their friends, their parents and family still have the most significant impact on their development. Consistent and healthy family relationships offer children the security to develop and learn. Children in this age group will often make mistakes, but they need parents who understand that errors are just part of the learning process.

Children at this age are more malleable compared to teenagers and generally take a great deal of notice of their parents' thoughts and opinions. So, take the time to influence your child's thinking and values, while also mirroring back to them that they are capable of doing their own thinking as well.

The lives of children in this stage are dominated by rules and routines. It is through rules that they learn right from wrong, and how to behave. Later in the stage they start to think in terms of rights and responsibilities, which are more abstract concepts.

Many children in this stage will develop a strong sense of justice and can become incensed when a sibling, friend or teacher treats them or others unfairly.

A primary-school-aged child becomes more capable physically, socially and academically. From my experience he is far more competent than most adults think. For too long we've under-estimated what they are capable of doing and so often expect too little of them in regards to looking after themselves, looking after others and moving independently around their neighbourhood.

During the latency stage, children become very social and are able to hold conversations with others outside their usual interests. They benefit from spending time alone with their parents, as well as spending time with their whole family. Children at this stage are trying to negotiate many new social situations at school; they can, however, be faulty observers and are prone to misinterpret the intentions of others. They need parents who can help them inter-pret accurately what may be happening and also help them process their feelings and thoughts about their new experiences.

Independence

Now is the time, if you haven't already done so, to insist your kids help at home without being paid. While not all children in a family will help in the same way the expectation that they 'pull their weight' should be established.

Children in this stage have an outward orientation and are exploring their place in the world. Most of their parents enjoyed the type of childhood described by Lenore Skenazy in her book *Free-Range Kids* but, as discussed earlier, this spoonfed gener-ation doesn't have the same freedom to roam. There are many reasons for this, including: organised childhoods that leave little free time for roaming; greater parental nervousness and adversity to risk; and a redesign of neighbourhoods away from the corner-shop model to a centralised shopping-centre model that leaves little opportunity for kids to carry out the sort of errands that past generations did routinely. This is an age and stage for greater neighbourhood exploration, for taking on real responsibility and for developing personal confidence and efficacy before adolescence starts.

From self-help to self-management

Your goal as a parent should be for your child to be completely self-managing by the end of primary school. That is, he can get himself and others up each morning; make his own breakfast; prepare his own schoolbag; collect his own school uniform; put any notes under your nose to be signed and returned to school; and so it goes on. Now, that doesn't mean that kids will do all this all the time, because other factors come into play such as busy schedules and early starts. Children will need some assistance at times; however, it's good to keep in mind that, when left to their own devices, they generally do remarkably well at organising their daily tasks. Sometimes they just need the opportunity.

Involve them in mealtimes

Mealtimes are the fulcrum around which healthy families operate. A shared meal is more than food. It's a ritual that binds people together; it's a vehicle for parents to influence their children; and it's an expression of love and care. It is also fundamental to children's wellbeing because there is a strong correlation between good mental health in young people and those who regularly share a family meal. Mealtimes also offer plenty of opportunities for children to help, including running errands, preparing the meal, setting the table, clearing the table, packing the dishwasher and other jobs. There's something for everyone!

Use pocket money to develop independence

A regular allowance is a fabulous way to promote real independence in children. Start in lower primary school and gradually increase their allowance the older they become. Importantly, you need to increase the areas that their allowance covers. For instance, in lower primary school a child's pocket money might go towards the purchase of some sweets and one or two other items each week. However, in middle primary school it might increase to cover the cost of one or two lunch orders each week, their bus money and some treats. In later primary school it could even cover some of their clothing purchases as well. The important thing is not to cover for kids if, for instance, they don't budget appropriately and run out of money for school-canteen lunches. They can either make their own lunches at home or perhaps borrow from a sibling and repay out of their next allowance. Pocket money used well is a fantastic way to develop independence in kids.

Look after pets

It's a quirk of life that most children want a pet, but they just don't want to look after it in the long term. Many kids discover that, following the initial flush of enthusiasm, looking after a pet can be a grind – walking the family pooch, cleaning out the guinea-pig cage, or feeding the family feline. But pet care offers priceless lessons in the development of grit, responsibility and nurturance – all necessary attributes for independent success.

Grit

Grit is developed when kids work through hard, boring stuff or difficulties. It's neurological as well as psychological as it impacts the brain. Looking after a pet is often boring and monotonous, which is a good lesson to learn.

Responsibility

What does your child do that someone else relies on? Smaller families often mean fewer chances to show your reliability and responsibility. Pet ownership comes with real built-in responsibility. You don't have to create it. You just have to insist that they keep to their end of the bargain – to look after their pet.

Nurturance

Having a pet gives kids a measure of control and allows them to care for something just as their parents (and older siblings) care for them. Children's nurturance needs to be . . . nurtured.

Walk, ride or take public transport to school

The opportunity to go to school on your own was a luxury that previous generations enjoyed. While it may have seemed at the time like something simply to be endured, most people I discuss this matter with look back with fondness and nostalgia. For most people it meant freedom, friendship and fun. For a short time each day kids experienced a delicious type of freedom away from both teachers and parents – a time to muck about, dawdle and mess around with mates. It also gave kids some familiarity with their neighbourhood. It's well established that currently more children are driven to school than ride or walk, which denies children the same opportunity for friendship, fun and freedom. Busy schedules, less child-friendly neighbourhood layouts and working parents are just some of the reasons that prevent kids walking to school. If possible, look for ways to allow your child to get to school on their own. It's fantastic for their independence and wellbeing. If children are too young, walk or ride with them some of the way until they are old enough and skilled enough to make the trip without you.

Private! Keep out!

Did you build a fort or a cubby when you were a child? Many parents I know speak with misty-eyed enthusiasm about the hideouts that they built. Most recall a special place that few, if any, adults knew about. And they were having fun – so much fun, they wouldn't for a second spare a thought that it was good for them, and contributing to their ability to flee the family nest at a later age.

Educator David Sobel from Antioch University New England has conducted a study of children's fort play, and he's found that it's not just a random act of play. Children the world over organise special places that they can retreat to away from the adult world. These private worlds can be anywhere – in suburban backyards, basements, in sheds, behind sheds, up trees, under hedges, in the bush – any space that kids can crawl into and cover over will do.

According to Sobel the urge to create forts starts at age five or six and ends at around twelve, which is about the time they start to look in the mirror and realise they are too old for that sort of stuff.

It is developmental, because it frequently starts inside with children as young as three putting blankets over tables or the backs of chairs and using blocks and boxes to create their own little hidey places. The next step, sometime in primary school years, is to move outside away from parents' view. It's then that the fun and complexity ramps up a level or two. Old lumps of wood are found, tools are borrowed and the construction begins!

So, what's this fort-building all about? It's about helping kids step away from the safety and security of their own home. But it also gives kids a chance to control their own environment; to use their imagination; and put up a defence against the outside world. It's their space – it belongs to them!

Traditionally parents did nothing to encourage cubby-building. Kids naturally went outside or they were sent out and they scrounged whatever they could and away they went. It's hard to kick-start cubby-building, but it could help to: get kids outside more often; provide them with materials for fort-building; make sure they have some room and space to explore; respect their privacy and, as the sign says, Keep Out!

I really think the trick is to try not to organise it. You can nudge them a bit but that's about all. If the theory holds, and I reckon it does, with some time and space they'll know what to do.

Resilience

The developmental task for children in this age group is to work out what they can do and how they can fit in, so naturally they have an outward orientation. This inevitably means that they will experience many social challenges, disappointments, frustrations, hardships and inconveniences. How they navigate through these challenges will depend on many factors, including the severity of the incident, their spirit, their attitude and the attitude and support of the significant adults in their life. This is the stage to put some experiences in your children's resilience bank accounts that will build up their internal resourcefulness in the future.

Give kids a chance to resolve their social challenges

It's during latency that children develop the skills to resolve their own problems and also learn how to regulate and manage their emotions. With this in mind it's wise for parents to resist the urge to solve their children's problems and challenges.

Most social problems that children experience revolve around conflict, rejection or exclusion. Each can be painful for a parent to bear. React empathetically when your kids are upset. That means that you stop and really listen.

'I get it,' is the most helpful response you can give a child of any age who is upset by the actions of others – but it must be genuine. My guess is that you've experienced a similar situation to one that has distressed your child, so just think back and *you'll get it*! You'll be responding on a feeling level.

But that doesn't mean that you act . . . yet. If you do you'll be reacting to your feelings, and if you've ever acted out of anger with your child, you'll know that doing as you feel isn't always wise.

So, what to do after you show your understanding? When emotions have settled, ask good questions to find out if a dispute is a one-off event or an ongoing issue. Ascertain your child's part in the situation and, importantly, do your best to understand if your child has the power or the wherewithal to resolve the problem. If you think that there is nothing they can do to resolve a continuing dispute, then it may be time to advocate on your child's behalf by initiating a meeting with a teacher, carer or coach. If you think your child can resolve this themselves, give them the time, space, ideas and encouragement they need to manage conflict.

Managing bullying

Bullying is a common behaviour experienced for the first time by children in this age group.

According to the 2009 Australian Covert Bullying Prevalence Study one in four kids from Years 4 to 9 experiences some type of bullying at school. Frequent bullying is highest in Year 5 (32 per cent experiencing some bullying) and Year 8 (29 per cent), so it is something that parents and teachers need to understand.

Bullying is an insidious behaviour that transgresses children's right to feel safe and secure. It can adversely affect children's learning, further peer relations and their emotional wellbeing.

Often children will tease, argue and sometimes fight, which shouldn't be confused with bullying. Bullying is selective and intentional. It's also repetitious rather than a one-off or occasional event. It can be physical, verbal or social exclusion. It also now happens online, which means some kids no longer feel safe at home. Kids generally feel powerless when they experience bullying.

Bullying is an issue to be discussed around the meal table, in the context of keeping kids safe. It's best broached within the context of personal safety, so discuss with your child his right to feel safe; how to know when he feels unsafe; and what to do if he experiences or witnesses bullying.

Knowing when kids are being bullied

Some research suggests that around 20 per cent of bullying goes unreported, so it can be difficult to spot children who experience bullying. However, kids will usually show signs in three ways:

1. **Acting out:** Look for outward signs such as displays of unusual aggression at home, talking about hating school and getting into trouble more often.
2. **Acting in:** Be on the lookout for subtle behaviour changes such as sullenness, withdrawing from usual activities, being uncommunicative, feigned illness, bed-wetting and altered sleep patterns.
3. **Telltale signs:** You may notice more obvious physical signs such as torn clothes, items missing, altered school routes and physical injuries.

Children who are bullied usually display a combination of signs. Children often find it hard to communicate that they are being bullied. Some don't have the language required. Many kids feel ashamed, or even believe what bullies tell them. Sometimes kids are also reluctant to tell adults about bullying because they fear that they will take the matter out of their hands, so your approach needs to be gentle and non-judgmental.

Here are six things to do if you suspect your child is being bullied.

1. **Listen to their story:** It really is important to stay calm and get the real story. Kids need to be believed when they are bullied, so make sure they get the chance to talk.
2. **Get the facts:** Bullying behaviour usually follows patterns. An accurate picture will help you determine your next course of action; for example, whether you need to teach your child some

avoidance or coping strategies or gain assistance from your child's school.

3. **Recognise and validate their feelings (anger, fear and sadness are common)**: Bullying always elicits strong feelings, so make sure kids can share their thoughts and feelings with you.

4. **Give them some common coping skills and defence mechanisms:** Look for simple ways to help them handle the bullying, such as making sure they stay in pairs, practising a comeback line or even walking and talking confidently.

5. **Get the school involved:** If your child continues to struggle with bullying, contact their school. Resist the temptation to confront suspected bullies, or their families. Teachers generally have very practical, tried and true ways to tackle bullying.

6. **Help build your child's support networks and their self-confidence:** Positive peer groups are great protective factors for kids when they are bullied, so do all you can to encourage and build their friendship groups inside and outside school.

Parents of children who are bullied frequently also need someone to talk to. Not only is this good for your mental health but it helps keep issues in perspective as well.

Now's the time to develop good mental-health habits

It seems strange to talk about promoting good mental health in children.

Shouldn't all children naturally have good mental-health habits? After all, childhood is supposed to be a relaxed time of life, free from the pressures and stresses that come hand in hand with adulthood.

Sadly, it doesn't seem that way. According to the Australian Psychological Society one in seven Australian children experience some type of mental-health issue, with ADHD, anxiety and depression being the most common.

Having good mental health doesn't mean kids don't experience difficulties or worries. Feeling worried, sad or fearful is normal. Kids who are mentally healthy are equipped to handle many of life's curve balls that come their way. They also don't let their emotions overwhelm them. As a result they learn better and have more friends.

It's during latency that parents need to begin developing good mental-health habits to last into adolescence and beyond.

Sleep

Sleep is one of the building blocks of mental health and wellbeing. Many children and just about all teenagers are sleep-deprived at the moment. (Many parents are sleep-deprived as well!) Children need between ten and twelve hours' sleep to enable proper growth and development, while teenagers need a minimum of nine hours. One of the single most powerful strategies to improve kids' abilities to cope with stressful or changing situations is to ensure they get enough sleep.

Exercise

When my mum would tell me all those years ago to turn the television off and go outside and play, she didn't know she was promoting good mental health. She just knew that physical activity was a good thing for an active growing boy. Kids today get less exercise than those of past generations, which is an impediment to mental health. Exercise stimulates the chemicals that improve mood and release the stress that builds up over a day. An hour's movement per day seems the minimum for kids. How much exercise does your child do?

Creativity

Kids should practise creativity if for no other reason than it helps them experience the state of 'flow'. This is the state of getting so immersed in an activity that you forget about time and place. Writers and other creatives understand the concept of flow. It's energising and helps take stressed and worried kids out of themselves.

A space of their own

Children of all ages benefit from having some space of their own where they can think. Quiet time and down time give boys the chance to let their thoughts wander around inside their head. They also help them get to know, and even like, themselves. Boys will often do their best thinking on their own, so they tend to retreat to their cave (bedroom) when things go wrong at school or in their relationships. They need to go within to find their own answer.

Relaxation

Make sure your child has a hobby or activity that relaxes them. The ability to relax and get away from the stresses of everyday life is essential. Some children who have real difficulty switching off may benefit from practising meditation or mindfulness, but most kids just need time to chill out so they can relax naturally. (I personally practise mindfulness and have found it a really helpful way to turn off my brain for a while!)

Weekend routine

Have two routines – weekday and weekend. Most households are pretty highly scheduled these days. There are routines for getting up, coming home, eating meals and going to bed. These structures are necessary when we're busy. Families need a second, more relaxed weekend routine that helps kids unwind. It's important to have this release valve if families are flat-out busy during the week.

Volunteering

Social isolation is a huge predictor of poor mental health. Encourage your child to be connected to and help others in any way possible. Helping others reinforces social connectedness and the importance of being part of a community, as well as providing opportunities for positive recognition.

Accountability

Kids in the primary-school years benefit from having a real responsibility that other people in the family rely on. Whether it's unpacking a dishwasher, hearing younger siblings read or walking the family dog, they should have an activity that no one else will step in and do. If you want your child to be responsible, you need to give them responsibility. In many families responsibilities go to the most capable, frequently the eldest child, while those who can really benefit from being given real jobs are neglected. This has the effect of overburdening the eldest or most capable, and making other children dependent.

Teach responsible behaviour

Children in this stage are learning how to be social and how to fit into different groups and with different teachers. It's a stage in which you can begin to develop self-regulation and self-control in your kids, which is linked to long-term success. Discipline at this age needs to be consistent; it should have a teaching focus and be based on respect.

Make manners a priority

The use of good manners is respect in action, so spend time teaching and reminding your child to use social conventions such as 'please' and 'thank you' when appropriate. This will help them learn to treat others respectfully.

Use consequences

This is the time to use logical and natural consequences to teach your kids to take personal responsibility for their behaviour.

Talk through problems together

Your child is now old enough to talk to about their behaviour. The two of you can start to solve problems together. Discuss the behaviour you expect without using guilt or shame to control your child.

Recognise good behaviour

During this stage your recognition and attention is usually a significant driver of what kids regard as acceptable behaviour. Make sure you let them know when you are pleased with their behaviour.

Make sure they make amends

It's during this age that children should be encouraged to make amends when they have transgressed the rights of others. 'Do you forgive me?' is far more powerful than merely offering an apology when they have hurt someone. This is an age when real account-ability for poor behaviour needs to be reinforced, so avoid letting them off the hook if they've transgressed the rights of others, and use behavioural consequences to keep them accountable.

Integrity

As children move into the primary-school years their focus is increasingly on peer relationships. It's in this context that integrity is taught and also tested. 'Doing the right thing' is relatively easy at home when a child has only his parents and siblings to consider, but trickier when he has to negotiate associations with other children who may or may not share his values. This requires increasingly that children make the right choices when you are not around, which is a test of their character and, to an extent, also your parenting where you teach children right from wrong.

Give children experience in decision-making

It's important to give children experience in their own family to make some decisions for themselves so that they are capable of making smart choices at school and beyond. In healthy families decisions occur in three ways.

Parents rule

Parents as wise leaders with children's best interests at heart make decisions for kids about issues such as health, safety, education and kids' wellbeing. You may take your five-year-old's ideas on board about his schooling but you decide the school that he goes to.

Kids decide

Usually parent help is needed, but there are some issues that kids can decide. This will differ for many families but I personally like to give kids latitude over bedroom tidiness, the amount of food they eat, how they spend pocket money, what they wear, their choice of leisure, and the like.

Family discusses

There are times when everyone has some input into how the family operates. Kids have input into routines, sorting out joint problems (for example, what to do with wet towels left on the floor) and family rules, including how mobile phones, televisions and computers are used.

It's in these contexts that children get experience making choices and also develop the capabilities to help them recover from a poor choice. Also by being involved in family discussions children learn how their choices, and subsequent behaviours, affect others.

Discuss friendships with children

For many children and parents the biggest threat to behaving with integrity comes from interactions with peers. Your child may know right from wrong but when she is around her peers this knowledge can disappear, particularly if popularity is a challenge for your child. It helps to be open and frank in your conversations about friendships; in particular, discuss the times children will feel uncomfortable about some of their friends' suggestions about appropriate behaviour. For instance, how will your child react when a friend suggests they watch a video you wouldn't approve of; they go to places where they feel unsafe; or a friend says hurtful things to other children? Help your child recognise when the behaviour or action of others is wrong. Either use a rational filter – such as, the behaviour steps on the rights of others to be treated fairly – or an emotional filter, where kids recognise an uncomfortable gut reaction. Then discuss what they may say or do when they feel compromised or uncomfortable with possible behaviours that friends suggest.

Does too much praise encourage compliance?

One of the adverse effects of excessively praising children, particularly for their good or compliant behaviour, is that it can cause them to continually seek the approval of other people. Nothing wrong with that per se but it can be a problem if a child behaves in ways that always please others, either subjugating their own needs or the rights to fair treatment of others. For example, a compliant girl may be nasty to another girl just to curry favour or do the dirty work of a peer whom she wants as a friend. In our desire as parents to raise good kids we need to be careful not to confuse compliance with assertiveness, particularly when we want kids to stand up for what is right and act with integrity.

Self-confidence

In many ways these are the prime confidence-building years. Some kids' confidence levels fall when they start school, finding themselves in unfamiliar situations with new children to meet and new rules to learn. Self-confidence is an area that parents have significant influence on, particularly with children of primary-school age and younger.

As a parent, you are in the prime position to mirror back to your kids how they should see themselves. You do this through your messages, your expectations and the way you treat your child.

Confidence comes from overcoming fears and being brave; however, many children during this stage avoid taking social or learning risks. Your child will benefit from having at least one parent who can really encourage them to take risks, meet new challenges and not be held back by self-doubt and fear.

Children in this age group will often meet with discouragement and disparaging comments from their peers. An encouraging, affirming parent is the best antidote to these.

Practical confidence-building strategies include: moving from praise to encouragement; teaching kids to self-praise; encouraging them to think for themselves; challenging them with real respon-sibility; and helping them spend time in activities where they experience success.

Developing a growth mindset in your kids

Perhaps the most exciting news in the parenting area over the past decade is the discovery of brain plasticity. That is, the brain is always growing and developing as opposed to it developing and reaching its nadir at a certain age; and then it's all downhill from there.

Current thinking supported by research shows that people who believe they can increase their intelligence through effort and challenge actually get smarter and do better in school, work, and life over time. They know that mental exercise makes their brains grow smarter – the same way that physical exercise makes an athlete stronger and faster. And they are always learning new ways to work smarter and build their brains.

It's exciting to know that your child's talent and smarts are not fixed. Their brain can always learn more, continue to grow and be stretched. This doesn't mean that your child doesn't have a propensity to be skilled. Genetics gifts us with certain abilities that are either developed or they're not. Instead, your child's abilities and talents, just like yours, evolve over time.

So, as a parent it seems smart that you should develop a growth mindset in your child. A fixed mindset is limiting, even debilitating for kids. You want them to believe that with effort and practice they can develop their skills and abilities in whatever area or interest they wish to pursue. If they believe that intelligence and talent is fixed, those beliefs will become self-fulfilling prophecies. Once again, it all comes down to attitude!

Jenny Brockis in her wonderful book *Future Brain* reminds us that success has more to do with fluid intelligence, tenacity and belief. She writes, 'Our attitude or mindset is not something we are born with. It evolves gradually, refined by our experiences and who we spend our time with.'

Carol Dweck, author of *Mindset: The New Psychology of Success*, believes that a growth mindset is the quality that separates those who succeed from those who don't. Her research reveals how the use of language when praising kids can have a profound impact on their attitudes. Subtle differences in tone, wording and phrasing can lead even a child at two-and-a-half to have self-limiting beliefs when they start school a few years later.

The problem with praising intelligence and ability is that it leads to fixed-mindset development. Kids believe that their success relies on their ability or talent, rather than their effort or attitude. So, to be respected and recognised as successful, they become risk-averse. Far better to achieve some success no matter how meagre, than risk failure and be seen as dumb, stupid or a failure.

So, how can a parent develop a 'growth mindset' in children?

Praise effort over results

Effort is seen as central to developing a growth mindset, so focus your comments on the processes of what kids do rather than results. Statements that link children's success to their effort reinforce the notion that success comes from something other than natural ability, talents or smarts.

Comments such as, 'You worked hard to get that right!', 'It's amazing what fifteen minutes of practice every day will do to your spelling!' and 'Your shooting for goal is so much more accurate. Have you been practising?' are teaching statements because they provide information that children can use in the future.

But Dweck recently pointed out that focusing on effort alone is not enough to build a growth mindset. Moreover, we can't just praise kids for effort if they aren't getting positive results anyway – that just leads to frustration.

Praise strategy as well

While effort is key for achievement, it's not the only thing. Kids need to try new strategies and seek input from others when they're stuck. They need this repertoire of approaches – not just sheer effort – to learn and improve. Adults need to discuss strategy and ways to improve that are meaningful. It helps too to focus language on better and smarter ways of improving. Comments such as 'That was a smart idea to tackle the hardest task while you were fresh!' (strategy) and 'You recognised the first few steps were the most important but then after that you were right' are descriptive statements that have significant instructional value for kids.

Give honest feedback

Providing your child with honest feedback about their performance not only helps them improve, but also promotes a growth mindset. We often shy away from giving feedback for fear of harming children's self-esteem, but confidence can be maintained when we are sensitive in the way we provide it. For instance, focusing on two or three things a child does well before giving constructive feedback is one way you can keep a young learner's head up while giving pointers about better performance.

Look for opportunities to stretch your child's capabilities

Encourage kids to stretch their capabilities by adding depth and breadth to their list of activities. Boys, in particular, often invest all their time in areas such as sport or online gaming to develop their talents over time. Encourage them to push themselves across a range of areas. Conversely, encourage a child who dabbles in many areas or interests without specialising in any, to go deeper in one area.

Harness the power of 'yet'

Got a child, particularly a preschooler, who shouts in defiance or frustration, *'I can't do it!'*? This is a definitive statement, which indicates feelings about the present. By responding to such a statement with, *'You can't do it yet. You're still learning. Keep trying,'* you are moving a child toward future possibility. The word 'yet' reframes the sentence away from present frustration or inability toward a future possibility. Dweck claims the word 'yet' helps children see themselves on the learning curve, and is related to persistence and greater confidence. *Sesame Street*, the iconic US program aimed at skilling up preschoolers, promotes this theme and includes the song 'The Power of Yet' in its regular repertoire.

Tell stories of resilience

Storytelling is a powerful way of shaping children's understanding of how the world works. According to a recent study, children who hear stories about how families members overcome obstacles are more resilient and display more grit in the face of challenges. The most helpful stories are those that are realistic, reflecting life's ups and downs. It's often stories of difficulty rather than success that teach and inspire children to persist. Similarly, it helps to remind children of times they worked hard to overcome an obstacle. These may range from learning how to ride a bike to sticking with a puzzle or adjusting to a new sibling in the family.

Having a plastic brain means that we can continue to acquire new skills, learn new things and embed new habits across our lifespan. It is important, then, that we help children develop a growth mindset so that they can reap the benefits of brain plasticity over their lifetime rather than be limited by their belief systems.

Ten growth-mindset statements

If you find yourself or your child using fixed-mindset statements, replace them with statements that promote growth. Here are some examples.

Fixed mindset	Growth mindset
I'm no good at this.	What do I need to do to get better?
I give up.	I'll try a few more things.
This is too difficult for me.	This will take some work.
I'm a hopeless speller.	I have to work hard at my spelling.
I always muck up.	Learning new things takes time.

I'm so dumb!	I do some silly things sometimes.
That's good enough.	Is this my very best work?
I'm smart, so I'll pass.	When I apply myself I'll pass.
I'm a natural at most sports.	I can get better at most sports.
That didn't work.	Now let's try plan B.

Emotional intelligence

Latency is the time when parents can start to teach their children how to recognise and regulate emotions. It can be difficult for children of all ages to recognise and articulate how they feel, so they can benefit from having a concrete aid to help them. The best tool I've seen for helping kids build this type of emotional intelligence is the Mood Meter, developed by the team at the Yale Center for Emotional Intelligence under the stewardship of Professor Marc Brackett.

The Mood Meter

The Mood Meter is a research-based tool that assists children and parents to regularly recognise and label their moods; decide whether to maintain their mood or shift their state; and keep a record of their feelings and moods over time. The visual nature of the Mood Meter is particularly useful for boys, who are more likely to be highly visual by nature.

Let's look at how the Mood Meter works.

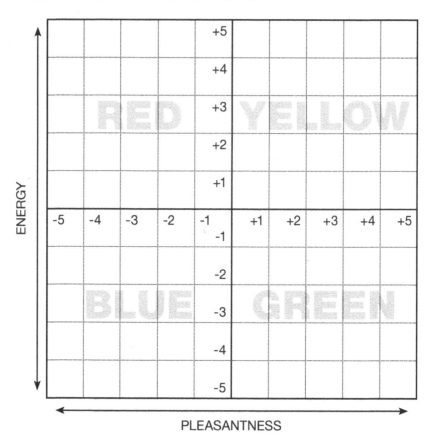

The horizontal axis refers to pleasantness of feelings. The further right along this axis the more pleasant the feelings are. As we move to the left, the feelings are less pleasant. The vertical axis refers to arousal or energy levels. The bottom of the axis refers to low energy, while the further up the axis the more feelings of energy and arousal you feel. When the two axes meet, four quadrants are created.

Top right-hand quadrant – the yellow zone

Look at the top right-hand quadrant bound by high pleasantness and high energy. This is the quadrant of energy, excitement and enthusiasm. It's a pleasant place but it's also highly energised. It's a great place to be in. We tend to feel good, feel well and feel on top of things. Words that go in this area include: pumped, joyful, inspired, positive, content, lively, cheerful, playful, awesome, ecstatic. This zone is signified by the colour yellow.

Bottom right-hand quadrant – the green zone

If you move down the vertical axis and into the bottom right-hand quadrant you've moved into the green zone. This is the quadrant where calmness, contentment and comfort lives. It's the zone you generally want to be in once your working and parenting day is done. It's the place of chilling out and relaxing. It's a pleasant but not necessarily productive place to be. If we spend all our time here not much will get done. Words that go in this area include: placid, peaceful, easygoing, secure, happy, balanced, carefree, playful, grateful and serene. This zone is signified by the colour green.

Bottom left-hand quadrant – the blue zone

Move left across the vertical axis and you are in the low-energy and unpleasant-feeling quadrant. Disappointment, discouragement and despondency but also reflection, empathy and concern live here. This zone is a place we often don't feel comfortable in, but simply being human means that we will become accustomed to it, whether we want to or not. Words that go in this area include: unhappy, dull, blue, down, sad, shattered, melancholy, lonely, depressed, despair. This zone is signified by the colour blue.

Top left-hand quadrant – the red zone

Above the horizontal axis and to the left of the vertical axis lies the red zone, where anger, anxiety and annoyance live. This is a zone containing unpleasant feelings, although it's different to the blue zone because a person here also experiences significant energy levels. They are certainly not sleepy or solemn. They are feeling quite activated and usually ready for action. Words that go in this area include: peeved, vexed, troubled, irritated, annoyed, nervous, upset, passionate, ferocious, enraged. This zone is signified by the colour red.

Introducing the Mood Meter to children

The Mood Meter is a great tool when it's in the hands of your children. There are many ways children can use the Mood Meter depending on their age, experience and interest.

Check in

Encourage your child to check in on the Mood Meter at least twice a day. On a piece of paper encourage him to write the feeling and give a reason he feels this way, and place it in the Mood Meter. (For example, 'I feel mad because Astrid took my bag. Monday 8.05am.' Or, 'I'm nervous because I'm speaking in front of the whole school at assembly. Wednesday 8.10am.') Sometimes kids can't give a reason and that's fine. Don't push it.

Reinforce the four zones through stories and books

When reading stories to children point out the zones that different characters may be in at different times during a story. The same opportunity to identify feelings can arise while watching television or a movie. Ask kids about the appropriate zones certain characters would be in on the Mood Meter following various experiences.

Place a Mood Meter in a prominent place

Make sure there is a Mood Meter prominently displayed so the whole family can refer to it when appropriate. The visual nature of the Mood Meter makes it a wonderful tool.

chapter thirteen

Age ten to fifteen – The awkward years

A snapshot of this stage

These are years in which children have one foot in childhood and one foot in adolescence. It's a transition stage – for children *and* their parents. The task for young adolescents is to establish an identity separate from their parents. This identity formation begins during puberty, and doesn't finish until well into the twenties for most young people.

Young adolescents wage an internal battle between the child inside and the emerging teen. The realisation that they have left the world of childhood and all it represents can lead to great sadness. Many young people wear two faces – an adult face full of false bravado for the outside world, and a childlike face that emerges in the privacy of their own bedroom and occasionally in front of their parents and family. Some children in this age group can be found secretly playing with a toy or doll from their early childhood.

Looking ahead can be scary for this group, because they know that some big decisions await them about a whole range of real-life issues, many of which may be beyond their current grasp. Everything in their environment pulls them toward adolescence. The media, their peers and even their parents are telling them that it is time to grow up – but inside, a part of them wants to stay young.

Many young people struggle during this period. Boys, in particular, fight their physiology and can become very awkward, self-conscious and even withdrawn. Girls usually mature earlier and often cope better with the transition, but negotiating friend-ships can be problematic.

This stage plays an important role in setting kids up for the next – upper teenage – phase. Steve Biddulph, in his book *Raising Girls*, refers to the stage as a time of 'intense preparation, not to be skipped over or rushed through'.

These are years when children start to question and challenge the unequivocal authority of their parents. Acquiescent children can become moody, quiet and uncooperative. It is during these years that young people realise that their parents have feet of clay. This can be hurtful to parents who formerly were a source of inspiration and font of wisdom. The 'my dad is bigger than your dad' taunt made by a six-year-old is replaced by 'my dad has more hang-ups than your dad' during this stage.

As a parent you will know that your child has entered adolescence as mood swings occur with both genders. These mood swings are caused by changes in levels of the dopamine hormone that affects feelings of wellbeing. When dopamine levels are low children seem to have a permanent type of 'gangster rap' stare. Excessively high dopamine levels can lead to quite manic behaviours and emotional outbursts. These mood swings signal the start of interesting times ahead for parents.

Early adolescents also display less interest in family activities and want to spend more time with their friends. They need freedom and structure at the same time. Their quest for independence needs to be tempered by parental supervision and monitoring of their behaviour and their emotional wellbeing.

During this period many children grapple with their physiology. For most, the onset of puberty occurs in late primary school, well before they have the emotional resources to cope with it.

The changing brain

This stage marks the beginning of the second of two growth spurts for your child's brain. When children are babies, their brain over-produces brain cells (neurons) and connections between those brain cells (synapses). It then starts to prune them back around the age of three. Much like the pruning of a tree, by cutting back weak branches others are allowed to flourish. The second wave of synapse formation shows a spurt of growth in the frontal cortex just before puberty (age eleven in girls, twelve in boys), which is then pruned back in adolescence. Even though the brain of a teenager between thirteen and eighteen is maturing, they are losing 1 per cent of their grey matter every year.

It may seem that having a lot of synapses is a particularly good thing, but the brain actually consolidates learning by pruning away synapses and wrapping white matter (myelin) around other connections to stabilise and strengthen them. The periods of pruning are as important for brain development as the periods of growth.

Leading brain researcher Jay Giedd, from the National Institute of Mental Health in Maryland, hypothesises that growth in grey matter followed by pruning of connections is a particularly important stage of brain development in which what young people in this stage do – or do not do – can affect them for the rest of their life. He calls this the 'use it or lose it principle'. He claims that 'if a teen is doing music or sport or academic work, those are the cells and connections that will be hardwired. If they're lying on the couch or playing video games or using social media, those are the cells and connections that are going to survive'.

Despite all this, with all the advances of science and the more technical knowledge we have about children, the best advice that most experts can give is the same as our grandparents were told generations ago – that parents need to spend loving, quality time with their children. The research shows that it's the relationships, the connections and the people in their lives that make the biggest difference to children. This is never more true than in these 'awkward years'.

Briefly, some other developmental changes you may notice as your child moves through young adolescence are:

- growth spurts that can lead to irritability and conflict;
- conflict between children and parents of the same gender;
- enormous sensitivity about body shape, growth and normality;
- teasing and bullying;
- a shift from wanting to spend time with parents and family to spending time with peers and friends.

Independence

Your young adolescent should be expected to help at home. However, consider giving them one or two significant weekly jobs, such as putting out the garbage, rather than continuing the same chores they were given during the previous 'latency' stage. More of the same doesn't always work with this age group.

The ultimate goal for an adolescent is to achieve autonomy from their parents. They are trying to do this at a tricky time, with their brain going through fundamental changes in the prefrontal cortex – the part of the brain responsible for rational decision-making, thinking things through and impulse control. As a result, you need to carefully support your child's journey to independence through this stage.

Establish fair family rules

Be clear about your expectations of their behaviour when they are not with you. Discuss the consequences of breaking these rules.

Help them understand the risks

Help your young person to assess the risks associated with increased independence.

Negotiate independence

Give your young adolescent the chance to negotiate greater independence by allowing them to prove to you that they are ready to have their boundaries pushed out.

Talk about values

Discuss values of fairness, tolerance and respect with your young person to help them formulate a sense of responsibility and a positive value system.

Scaffold to independence

This is the age when you can build 'scaffolds' to greater independence: allow your child to achieve increasingly greater autonomy, taking lots of small steps rather than one large step.

Allocate a meal each week for your young adolescent to prepare

You may help them at first, but eventually turn the responsibility over to them. If this is unworkable for you now, consider it something to work towards by the end of this stage. Kids in this age group are more than capable of preparing a meal, and you will find it a significant contribution to the family. It may need to fit in with busy schedules, but that's okay – your child will benefit from learning that they can in fact juggle a number of activities each day. Don't let them off the hook just because they are busy.

Give them an allowance

Young people increasingly want more power over their own life, and providing pocket money is one way to do this. Consider giving your young person enough allowance to cover clothing, mobile-phone bills, travel and school meals. Encourage them to budget, and set savings goals. This increase in autonomy will help your young person feel valued.

Resilience

Young adolescents are at increased risk of experiencing mental-health problems including anxiety and depression. If you're concerned about your child, see your GP, a school counsellor or health professional.

It is now time to make good mental-health habits a priority for your young person. Here are some ideas.

Maintain at least two friendship groups

Navigating social groups can be hard work for children at this stage. It helps to have a set of friends outside school to act as a buffer if friendship difficulties arise at school. Encourage your young person to maintain different friendship groups rather than opt for just one or two special friends.

Provide a space of their own

Young people of this age need a space of their own at home – somewhere that they can reflect on and process events. We all need this, but the need seems greater during this stage.

Talk about their troubles

A problem shared is a problem halved. Talking about what's worrying you is a great way to remove the burden and reduce anxiety. Gently encourage your child to be open with you, or to at least share their concerns with a trusted friend.

Develop their own interests

Make sure your young person has a hobby or activity that relaxes them. The ability to relax and get away from the stress of everyday life is essential.

Make sure they get enough sleep

Sleep is one of the building blocks of mental health and wellbeing. Just about all teenagers are sleep-deprived at the moment – along with many parents! One of the single most powerful strategies to improve a child's ability to cope with stressful or changing situations is to ensure they get enough sleep.

According to most sleep experts, the minimum amount of sleep a teenager needs for good mental health, wellbeing and learning is nine to ten hours per night.

The 'sleep clock' of approximately 75 per cent of young adolescents moves forward by up to 1.5 hours. In other words, they are not ready for sleep until much later. As our school starting times don't adjust to this, our adolescents are frequently operating on much less sleep than they need. To beat the frustration of sleeplessness, adolescents will often go online to entertain themselves, connect to social networks, play games or chat with their equally awake friends. This is counterproductive. Not only does the activity re-stimulate them, but the bright light from their digital screens delays the natural night-time build-up of melatonin, the hormone that makes us sleepy at night. By the time their body is finally ready for sleep, it will be even later than the 'natural' 1.5 hour difference.

If your young person complains of not being able to get to sleep, encourage them to read a book for a while, or listen to some (quiet) music. These activities won't exacerbate the problem.

Good sleep hygiene is one of the most important things you can impress upon your young adolescent during this developmental stage.

Accountability

Your approach to discipline during early adolescence needs to involve a mixture of firmness and compassion. Children in this age group are frequently placed in difficult situations by their peers, such as being asked to go out at night before they are ready. It can be a relief to have parents who place restrictions on them – it gives them someone to blame while maintaining their status. So, don't be afraid to take on the role of 'the bad guy'. Your child may not openly thank you, but secretly they may be relieved.

Most parents think their young adolescent is three years younger than they actually are, while the young person thinks they are three years older than they are. Discipline during this stage is about helping your young person be *safe* and *social* while allowing them to form a healthy identity separate from you.

Here are some ideas to help with discipline during this stage.

Set clear boundaries

Simple, clear boundaries around your child's behaviour such as home times, managing homework and the way they treat others are essential for this age group.

Reward responsible behaviour with greater freedom

Let responsible behaviour – rather than pressure from other teenagers – determine when boundaries are extended.

Use consequences to promote responsible behaviour

Most young adolescents will push parental and other adult-initiated boundaries. In some respects this is healthy, but they need to experience the consequences of any poor choices so that they can adjust their behaviour accordingly.

Stay calm

Consequences need to be delivered calmly to avoid conflict and also to make sure that your teenager takes the message on board.

Encourage reflection

Encourage your young person in this stage to think about their poor behaviour. Help them consider what led to the behaviour and how it might be avoided next time.

Give your teenager a voice

Agree together on consequences in advance. *'If you come home late what's a reasonable consequence, do you think?'*

Tell them how you feel

Use 'I' messages to let your child in this age group know how you feel about their behaviour. *'When you skip meals I really worry that you won't be able to do your best at school'* rather than *'What do you think you're doing not eating breakfast? What's going on?'*

Choose battles wisely

Sometimes we get into conflict with young adolescents over things that we can no longer control or that are relatively trivial. These can include their choice of clothing, how they spend their money and bedroom tidiness. It's a good idea to keep negative feedback to a minimum so that you can maintain a good relationship with your child through this period. Guide your young person around values, morals and relationships rather than fight about friendships, bedrooms and appearance.

Integrity

If integrity is taught in childhood, it's definitely tested in adolescence. The wish to comply and fit in with peers; the need to step away from traditional family values; and the internal changes a young person experiences – these all challenge their ability to act with integrity. 'Doing what's right' is hard during early adolescence.

Differentiate between friendships and cliques

Fellow parenting educator Catherine Gerhardt of Kidproof Australia says it's important for parents to talk with their daughters in the early teen years about friendships and staying true to their values and beliefs. In particular, we should discuss the difference between a friendship group and a clique. This can be helpful because many girls in the early teen years are conflicted by how they should treat others. Friends are those people with whom we share common interests and enjoy hanging out with, and who generally support each other. Friendship groups share similar values and beliefs and usually welcome new friends.

On the other hand, cliques are generally restrictive. They are usually ruled by a leader who sets the rules about who can be 'in' and how they should behave. Cliques usually exert a great deal of pressure to conform and often restrict members from forming friendships with people outside the group. In general girls are more inclined to want people to like them and have a greater desire to be accepted. It is important that we open up conversations around values and beliefs.

Boys can also experience cliques during early adolescence that can compromise their ability to act with integrity. While girls' cliques can be anti-social, many boys' cliques encourage behaviours such as smoking, drinking and risk-taking (truancy, train-surfing and even fighting). Loyalty is a high driver for many boys, causing them to conform with their mates even when they know they may be doing the wrong thing. Most teenage boys will act out of integrity when they are on their own, so talk to the individual rather than the group, and you are more likely to succeed in guiding a teenage boy.

It is also worthwhile to have a plan and build discussions around potential peer-pressure situations, such as alcohol, drugs or sex. Think ahead and discuss what young people can do when they are placed under pressure by peers. One simple phrase they can use when pressured by peers to act out of character is: 'No, not now!' This phrase buys some time and, importantly, allows a young person to save face with their peers.

Self-confidence

Confidence levels can vary greatly during this stage. Confidence and self-esteem are linked to many factors, including hormonal changes, how a young teenager thinks they look, how successful they feel, and how accepted they are by their peers and family. Young adolescents start to specialise in those areas where they experience success, and cease activities where they can't succeed or only achieve low status in the eyes of their peers. Loving, supportive family relationships can help insulate children in this age group against uncertainty, self-doubt and adverse peer relationships.

Encourage continually

Young people at this stage need a great deal of encouragement, because many live with uncertainty and self-doubt. Think back to how encouraging you were when your child was learning to walk and bring that same spirit into your parenting now.

Help your child rationalise, rather than exaggerate their worries

Young adolescents often jump to conclusions and catastrophise ('I'm hopeless!'), blaming themselves when they experience social problems or difficulties. Help your young person to work through their difficulties so they can rationalise and find solutions.

Help them find their spark

Kids in this age group need at least one activity or interest that they can form a positive identity around. They may need your help to identify it, but once that has been done support their efforts to pursue their new interest enthusiastically. This can sustain them during these rocky times.

Reassure and affirm

Remind your young person that self-doubt, mood swings and feelings of confusion are normal for this stage of development.

Point out the positives

This age group can traditionally present a gloomy picture to their parents, yet can be upbeat with their peers. Challenge gloom merchants to adjust their thinking and start to look for the positives in situations rather than focusing on the negatives.

Emotional intelligence

In the previous chapter I encouraged parents to introduce the Mood Meter to children as a tool to help them recognise, regulate and understand more about their emotional life. The Mood Meter is a great way to help early adolescents better understand what's happening to them during this turbulent period of brain-rewiring and subsequent mood swings. I encourage you to introduce the Mood Meter to your young person as a concrete way of helping them keep track of their emotions and also to build their emotional vocabularies.

Talk about emotions

It's my experience that many parents talk with their young people on a rational level rather than on an emotional level. In many families, *'What do you think?'* is heard more than *'How do you feel?'* You can encourage young people to open up simply by directing conversations to an emotional level. Whether you are talking about events involving them, or describing the impact of their behaviours on you or simply discussing everyday issues with them, you can direct the conversation toward the emotional impact that they have. One way to do this is to use 'I' statements when talking about their behaviour. A statement such as, *'I feel relieved when you come home on time'* informs a young person of the emotional impact of their behaviour on you. Similarly, you can hold a discussion about the rights and wrongs of bullying at school or you can discuss the emotional impact of bullying on the recipient, which encourages empathy as well as helping to build a more expansive emotional vocabulary.

Express yourself with the right words

Recently while riding on a tram I overheard two girls in their late teens talking. Referring to an exam she was about to take one girl simply said, 'I feel crap!' She repeated this on a number of occasions with no variation on vocabulary.

Her friend, on the other hand, said, 'I was feeling so anxious this morning that I felt sick when I got up. I went for a walk and I felt better. My little brother kept annoying me about this being my last exam and that I'd better not stuff it up. That made me feel really nervous, then I just began to feel irritated by him. I'm not feeling too bad now . . . just a little apprehensive but also a little excited that this will be my last exam! Whoa!'

One girl gave a running commentary on her moods that morning, including their causes and the subtle shifts. The second girl is clearly better equipped to manage her moods than the first girl; if, indeed, what I heard is a true representation of their emotional intelligence. I suspect it was. The message is simple: encourage young people to build a broad emotional vocabulary because the more nuanced their language the more readily they can shift their emotions.

Help them manage their feelings

Knowing that you may be feeling irritable is one thing, but knowing how to get yourself out of a funk is another matter entirely. Help your young person use healthy strategies such as taking some deep breaths to relax; changing their self-talk from

'I can't do this' to 'I know this material. I've been over it a number of times in school' before a test; to taking some time out to collect themselves and clear their mind before having a difficult conversation with a parent or teacher. There are a myriad ways that we use to get in the right mood for a task. Emotional intelligence means that young people have some skills at their fingertips to manage their moods when needed.

chapter fourteen

Age sixteen and beyond – The popularity and facing-up years

A snapshot of this stage

The age of sixteen is a time when social success takes precedence over academic success for many young people. Many schools battle for the hearts and minds of boys, in particular, during this period as the end of school and entry to the wider world is still a long way off.

Young people in this age group are stuck in a type of holding pattern, trapped between the world of childhood that they have left behind and the world of adulthood that they are still too young to enter. They are still a number of years from the independence that is available to eighteen-year-olds, yet they are constantly invited to act, think and behave as if they are older. Parties, alcohol and sexual freedom are just beyond the reach of many of these young people, yet like low-hanging fruit the former two, at least, are often readily available.

The quest for greater independence at this age, particularly at night, is often hampered by lack of public transport. Safety concerns prohibit many middle adolescents from travelling by train or bus at night, so they have to rely on adults to fill their transport needs.

It appears that the battle of wills is greatest between parents and young people in these years. It is during this period that many parents ponder the thought of someone else raising their young person for a while. A boarding school or even its modern equivalent – the overseas student-exchange program – is an attractive option for many.

Also around now the pathways through adolescence to adulthood diverge for girls and boys. Boys in this stage need to test themselves physically or intellectually as if to prove their worthiness. The sporting field can become a battleground as young men pitch themselves against opponents or against themselves as they strive to jump, run and battle harder. Girls tend to be more focused on negotiating relationships of all types, with friendships taking precedence over schoolwork. This can be frustrating for parents and teachers.

Adults outside the immediate family unit play an increasingly important role for adolescents during these years. It is a stage of life when grandparents have the opportunity to have a significant impact on the hearts and minds of young people. They can step forward to be part advisor, part mentor and part intermediary, sitting between an adolescent and his parents. Teachers, sports coaches and other members of the broader community can also play a part in mentoring or assisting young people during these difficult years. It's a time when 'sparents' – spare parents, including adult friends and relatives with or without their own kids – can step up and help parents out.

The fog of middle adolescence lifts as young people move toward the magic age of eighteen. This is a time when many begin to mature and face up to what has been happening to them. Cars, access to licensed premises and school completion are among the highlights that this group celebrates. But it is also a confusing time as they move into the unknown world of work or post-secondary education while, in many cases, not yet knowing who they are or what they want. The perceptions they had of themselves and the outside world when they were in school often don't quite match up with the reality.

Schools tend to minimise or hide the reality of failure from students. As these adolescents face a future away from the familiarity and security of school, for many it is the first time they encounter failure or really see where they stand according to objective measures. It can be a time when they receive a hefty reality check.

This group still needs a great deal of parental support; however, your parenting approach needs to change to be effective. Generations ago this cohort would have been entrenched in work and quite possibly have left home. Today they face far more uncertainty about their future as far as employment and education opportunities are concerned. One recent survey found that the average young person has changed their job three times by the age of thirty – a career or trade for life is no longer the norm. While many young people cope well during this period, others struggle and can spend a number of years trying to find out where their interests lie. One of the tasks for parents is to help their young adult discover their life goals and aspirations. This takes a willingness to mentor and provide emotional support.

Developmentally you may notice these things about this age group:

- Their social functioning in the adult world takes a dive around middle adolescence, but it returns toward the end of the secondary school years.
- They hold divergent views from you about a broad range of issues including politics.
- They may start to define themselves around the rules and mores of sub-groups.
- They experience tension between negotiating the world of peers and their personal life with school and family.
- They may instigate their own rituals and celebrations to mark their transition to adulthood.

Independence

While they live at home, young people should be required to contribute. Steven Biddulph, in his book *Raising Girls*, says: 'Doing things for others creates an inner shift.' He maintains that when young people help others, whether by cleaning the house or tidying up their bedroom, they gain feelings of pride, capability and freedom. Adulthood is about doing as much as being, so contributing at home is an adult thing to do.

The journey to independence continues, with girls being ready to move to autonomous adulthood well before boys. It seems the step to independent womanhood comes sometime between nineteen and twenty-five, while anecdotal evidence suggests that boys finally reach autonomous adulthood closer to twenty-seven.

This is the time to stop spoonfeeding young people and expect them to stand on their own two feet.

Treat your young person like a boarder

Once a young adult has left school but is still living in the family home, they should earn their keep and treat you respectfully, just as they would any landlord.

Build practical skills

Patiently teach life skills such as paying bills and filling in tax returns to develop real independence.

Step back and allow other adults in

Girls need many adult females in their life and boys benefit from contact with adult males other than their father. This helps them negotiate life away from their parents.

Keep the door open when they leave home

This is not so hard. The front door these days tends to be a revolving door, because it usually takes young people a number of attempts to leave the family nest.

Don't take on their problems

Your young adult needs to learn to stand on their own two feet, which can mean they experience some of life's hardships. These are all good learning experiences.

Encourage a part-time job

There are a number of benefits to a part-time job, regardless of how busy your young person is. First, earning their own allowance is one of their first steps toward real autonomy. Second, it's good for them to abide by rules set by someone other than their family and school. Third, being socially connected to a community group such as a workplace is a key contributor to good mental health and wellbeing.

Help your middle adolescent juggle work with other interests, and be supportive of them cutting work back if they are not coping or feel overwhelmed.

Resilience

Young people are at increased risk of experiencing mental-health problems including anxiety and depression. If you're concerned that your teenager is displaying any symptoms of a mental-health condition, see your GP, a school counsellor or health professional.

In this stage you need to continue to make good mental-health habits a priority for your young person. Here are some ideas.

Model good mental-health habits

Your teenager is now acutely aware of how you live your life and will be on the lookout for discrepancies between what you say and what you do. It's no use preaching good mental-health practices (see below) if you don't follow suit. I agree with my colleague, psychologist Andrew Fuller (author of *Tricky Kids* and many other books for parents), who maintains that parents need to teach their young people to live life well. Now is the time to do it.

Encourage exercise

Young people today get less exercise than those of past generations, which is an impediment to mental health. Exercise stimulates the chemicals that improve mood and release the stress that builds up over a day. An hour's movement per day is the minimum for kids.

Help them relax

Make sure your young person has at least one hobby or activity that relaxes them. The ability to relax and get away from the stresses of everyday life is essential. If your teenager has difficulty switching off they may benefit from practising meditation or mindfulness.

Watch out for alcohol and drugs

These are major risk factors for the development of mental-health problems in young people. Talk to your teenager about them. If you know they are using alcohol or drugs, discuss the risks and what they should be looking out for. If you are worried or concerned, see a health professional or a counsellor.

Make sure they get enough sleep

The minimum amount of sleep a teenager needs for good mental health, wellbeing and learning is nine to ten hours per night.

Accountability

Your approach to discipline during this stage needs to be a mixture of firmness and compassion, but increasingly it's about letting go. This is a gradual process, but it needs to happen.

Hand over power and responsibility to teenagers

Your middle adolescent is in the process of working out who they are – essentially, adolescence is a process of identity formation. The options for experimentation today can be overwhelming and much more lethal in consequence than in the past, which makes many parents more protective and controlling. You may need to work harder at easing your young person through this tricky time, but that doesn't mean that you should keep power and responsibility from your teenager. The handing over of power has to happen, and must be accompanied by the young person experiencing the consequences of their choices. It's only in this way that they can learn to improve or adjust their decisions and behaviours accordingly.

Set limits for identity formation

The focus of limit-setting should be on your teenager's needs, not your own parental-control needs. The best defence against bad decision-making is to give them practice making choices and solving some of their own problems. The best decision-making scenario is a cooperative one between your teenager and yourself, with them feeling comfortable discussing choices and incorporating some older, wiser parenting views. Provide options for your young person to choose from, within parameters. *'I am afraid you can't stay home on your own this weekend. You can either come with us, stay at Grandma's or stay at one of your friends' places. Let us know soon which one you want to do.'*

Use choices and consequences like a good cop

The key to using choices and consequences effectively is to use them like a good (read calm, dispassionate) cop, not a bad

258

or rude cop. It's not necessarily what you do and say but *how* you do and say things that will make the difference between success and failure in communicating with your middle-to-late adolescent.

Use a problem-solving approach individually

One way to help teenagers act more responsibly is to take a problem-solving approach. That is, you state the rule – *'I need you home safely by one o'clock'* – and then follow up with a statement that makes this a problem for both of you to solve: *'Let's come up with some ways to make this work for you and me.'* Then generate some ideas together, pick a solution and try it. Your teenager will often learn more about decision-making and identity formation from a bad decision made well than by simply going along with what they think you want. They will learn more by being allowed to choose poorly, such as the virtues of delaying gratification, the advantages of proper research and even the advantages of heeding advice.

There's a time and place . . .

You may find that your young person likes to negotiate with you on the run. They just love to catch their parents out with last-minute requests to go out or meet up with friends. Other times they are simply indecisive. You'll be more successful if you choose the right time and place to take a request from your teenager or to work through a problem with them. Make that time and place clear – and be insistent about it otherwise you may be wasting your breath.

Integrity

Integrity and trust go hand in hand during middle adolescence and adulthood. Most young people want to be trusted by their parents yet can forget that trust is earned rather than given. 'You don't trust me,' has become a generational catchcry when parents are bold enough to restrict young people's behaviour. The response from parents should be, *'Well, no. I don't blindly trust you to do the right thing by others or your family. I'll give you that trust when you show me that you deserve it.'* Direct and straight to the heart of the matter. When we blindly trust young people to act in the best interests of others and not expect anything in return nor hold them to account when they mess up we do them no favours. It's during this stage that young people learn how hard it is to act with integrity – to do what's right, not what's easy – and parents discover how hard it is to promote a sense of right and wrong in young people.

Self-confidence

Confidence comes from overcoming fears of not measuring up and by facing up to what it means to be an adult. During this stage young people need parents who don't pussyfoot around too much, who challenge them to step up and accept responsibility.

In days gone by, the age of fifteen or sixteen was when young people were kicked out and expected to make their way in the adult world. A lot of adult time and energy was put into preparing young people for adulthood in those days, accompanied by a great deal of ritual. Once the bridge to the adult world was crossed, there was no going back.

Your challenge today is to help your middle adolescent develop the practical competencies and emotional tools needed to move into adulthood.

Help them navigate rites of passage

Sadly for many young people today, the only significant rite of passage or ritual available is 'schoolies' week. However, many schools are now using formal 'rites of passage' programs to better help young people transition to adulthood. Some parents take on this challenge themselves by helping their teenagers define the type of person they want to be, and by beginning to treat them differently. Whether through a formal program or a family-initiated process, young people need some real recognition to help them make this step from childhood to future adulthood. A rite of passage won't make adulthood magically happen, but it will signal – to them, to you and to others – that a bridge has been crossed and there is no going back.

Teach living away from home skills

Invest time and energy into teaching your young person the multitude of skills he or she will need to live without you. Once they've left school their life changes, or should change, so they need to be able to fend for themselves, budget, complete a tax return, wash their own clothes, cook a meal and more.

Make sure they pull their weight

Resist the temptation to let your middle adolescent off the hook because they are tired or have a heavy workload at school. Insist they clean up after themselves, speak to others respectfully, apologise when they have done the wrong thing and otherwise behave as would an adult who is responsible for their actions.

Teach the power of choice

Real confidence comes when you know you can choose your response to different events. Teach your young person that they can change catastrophic thinking to rational thinking by changing their language. Teach them that they can be pleasant to others, even though those others may not be pleasant in return.

Don't let events define them

Middle adolescents can be at risk of being defined by one nasty remark from a peer or teacher, one failure at school or sport, or one awkward social encounter. Don't let your teenager corner the market on a label or personality type. This is an immature response to adverse events. Teach them that confidence comes from accepting yourself for who you are and looking within, to yourself, for self-acceptance.

Emotional intelligence

In previous chapters I looked at how you can develop emotional intelligence at different stages. I encourage you to revisit the earlier stages for ideas to help your young person identify and manage their emotions. The Mood Meter, which I introduced in Chapter 11, is relevant for teenagers and adults. In fact, I regularly use the Mood Meter to help me better understand the impact of stress on my emotions. It provides me with a snapshot of my moods, which enables me to make more informed decisions about how I manage stress and anxiety. In addition to using the Mood Meter you can promote emotional intelligence during this stage in the following ways.

Help them identify emotional triggers

When we are under duress our adrenal glands secrete a hormone called cortisol that enables us to become awake and aroused. After a stressful moment our body returns to normal. When we are always under stress our body continues to produce cortisol, which means we are in a continuous state of arousal. One way young people can reduce their levels of cortisol and thus lower the arousal state is to understand what triggers emotions in the first place. Triggers are individual by nature. Anger or anxiety are the main emotions that young people struggle with and it's these two that trigger the highest levels of cortisol. So, help young people to understand what triggered anger – usually accompanied by thoughts of injustice or fairness – and anxiety – usually accompanied by feelings of uncertainty, lack of control and obsessive thinking – in the first place.

Take a moment to manage anger and anxiety

When young people feel overwhelmed by emotion, encourage them to step away from the source of anger or anxiety and take deep breaths to change their thinking and their emotional state. Deep breathing is the only visceral activity that impacts thinking – it has a calming effect that changes thought patterns from exaggerating to rationalising. The hard part for a young person is to catch themselves before they act out – before delivering a rant, lashing out verbally or physically or sending that angry email.

Focus on developing long-term mental-health habits

This is a great life stage for young people to start to think about their long-term mental health and wellbeing activities, including the following.

Meditation

Spend five minutes each day focusing on breathing or repeating a simple mantra.

Physical activity

Participate in a variety of activities, including stretching, walking and other forms of exercise.

Entertainment

Embed entertainment in everyday life so that relaxation becomes a normal part of life.

Finding support

Encourage help-seeking behaviours by suggesting young people seek help or advice from family members, friends or professionals.

Goal-shifting

Help young people understand that good feelings come from shifting goals – from unrealistic to more workable or attainable goals.

Volunteering

The lifelong habit of service is as close to a guarantee of good emotional wellbeing as a young person is likely to find.

Conclusion

The premise of this book is simple – to encourage you to establish a mindset for developing kids' independence and to provide you with the blueprint to do so. Developing the independence mindset is relatively easy – you need to be on the lookout for opportunities to allow your child to develop autonomy at every stage of development. *'Is this something my child can do?'* is a question that we should constantly be asking ourselves when we resolve children's problems or carry out simple tasks that they can do for themselves, such as clearing away their plates after mealtime and getting themselves up in the morning. No spoonfeeding please!

Implementing this independence manifesto may be challenging for many readers. Developmentally, the prime time to start this process is in early childhood. So if your children haven't started school then they're at the ideal stage for independence-building, and following the methods outlined in this book should be relatively straightforward.

If your children have begun school or are in secondary school then you may have to change their existing habits. Expect some children to resist your attempts at promoting independence. After all, any child who has had a parent at his beck and call all his life is likely to resist any changes to the spoonfeeding ways he's used to. If you relate to this I suggest you make incremental changes rather than conduct a complete overhaul of your parenting. Start by implementing some simple self-help skills such as getting himself up in the morning or packing his own lunch for school. Progress to kids helping at home without being paid. When you feel confident you are on the right track look for new ways to make yourself redundant as a parent.

The central idea of independence-building that I've set out in this book is the most common sense way to raise kids. It's a recognition of the natural inclination for kids to prepare themselves to flee the family nest at the earliest and most convenient stage that has been lost over the last few decades. Adopting the parenting for independence blueprint will take parental courage as you may be swimming against the tide of popular parenting opinion that states a good parent is one that protects their children and ensures that they live a comfortable life. Parents who adopt the independence mantra know that to prepare children to live a productive, fulfilled life you need to start early and make sure kids are physically and emotionally equipped for the challenges as well as the joys that independent-living presents.

Parenting for independence also requires a different kind of parental courage. Standing back, letting go and giving kids freedom – all requirements for raising kids to be independent – mean that young people will inevitably risk experiencing failure, discomfort and hurt in the process. But accessing and facing risk has always been a part of childhood; it's only over the last few decades that much of the unpredictability and uncertainty has been removed from kids' lives, which keeps them dependent on adults for longer.

By applying the ideas outlined in this book you'll eradicate much of the fear and anxiety that blights the lives of so many children today. I'm not talking about developmental fears such as being separated from parents or being afraid of the dark. These are the types of fears that parents of all eras have had to contend with. I'm referring to fear of failure; fear of unfamiliar situations; fear of taking physical risks; fear of not being perfect and fear of rejection to name a few. All fears that percolate away when adults do too much for kids, expect too little from them and don't allow them to take social and physical risks. Our spoonfeeding ways do kids few favours.

I invite you to leave the spoon in the drawer where it belongs and aim for your child's early independence, which has always been the cornerstone of effective parenting. In doing so, you'll be preparing your child to take his place in a rapidly changing world that will reward those with the resilience to manage the inevitable ups and downs; the social and emotional skills to form strong, meaningful relationships and the propensity to do what's right, rather than what's easy, that comes with a strong sense of personal integrity.

Resources

Books

Adler, Alfred, *Understanding Human Nature*, Greenberg, New York, 1936

Balson, Maurice, *Becoming Better Parents*, ACER Third edition, 1989

Biddulph, Steve, *Raising Girls*, Finch Publishing, 2013

Brockis, Jenny, *Future Brain*, Wiley, 2015

Brown, Brene, *The Gifts of Imperfection*, Hazeldon, 2010

Dweck, Carol, *Mindset: The New Psychology of Success*, Ballantine Books, 2008

Fuller, Andrew, *Unlocking Your Child's Genius*, Finch Publishing, 2015

Fuller, Andrew, *Tricky Kids*, Finch Publishing, 2007

Grinder, Michael, *The Elusive Obvious*, Hawker Brownlow, 2011

Grose, Michael, *Why First Borns Rule the World and Last Borns Want to Change it*, Random House, 2003

Grose, Michael, *XYZ: The New Rules of Generational Warfare*, Random House, 2005

Grose, Michael, *Thriving!*, Random House, 2010

Grose, Michael, *A Man's Guide to Raising Kids*, Random House, 2000

Grose, Michael, *Great Ideas for Tired Parents*, Random House, 1996

Kagan, Jerome & Herschkowitz, Norbert, *A Young Mind in a Growing Brain*, Harvard University, 2005

Kluger, Jeffrey, *The Sibling Effect*, Riverhead Books, 2011

Preuschoff, Gisella, *Raising Girls*, HarperCollins, 2004

Seligman, Martin, *The Optimistic Child*, Houghton Mifflin, 2007

Skenazy, Lenore, *Free Range Kids*, Jossey-Bass, 2009

Sobel, David, *Children's Special Places: Exploring the Role of Forts, Dens, and Bush Houses in Middle Childhood*, Wayne State University Press, 1993

Articles, Websites & TV

'Australian Covert Bullying Prevalence Study', Cross D et al, Ecu Publications, 2011

Brackett, Marc, Yale Center for Emotional Intelligence

'Intrusive Parents Breed Self-critical Kids', *Asian Scientist*, 30 June 2016

'Life at 9', ABC TV, 2014

McCrindle, Mark, McCrindle Research

'The Australian Temperament Project', Australian Institute of Family Studies, AIFS publication, 2013